Mindset Makeover

*Understand the Neuroscience of Mindset,
Improve Self-Image, Master Routines for a
Whole New Mind, & Reach Your Full Human
Potential*

SOM BATHLA

www.sombathla.com

Your Free Gift

As a token of my thanks for taking out time to read my book, I would like to offer you a free gift:

Click Below and Download your **Free Report**

Learn 5 Mental Shifts To Turbo-Charge Your Performance In Every Area Of Your Life - in Next 30 Days!

You can also grab your FREE GIFT Report through this below URL:

http://sombathla.com/mentalshifts

Contents

Your Free Gift...2

Introduction 5

Chapter 1: Human Potential is Unknowable but Limitless 18

Chapter 2: Do You Know Your Mindset? 35

Chapter 3: Use Neuroplasticity- 5 Pillars to Redesign Your Mindset 51

Chapter 4: Building Self Image and Re-narrating Self-Talk 63

Chapter 5: Strategically Design Your Surrounding 82

Chapter 6: Effective Daily Routines to Empower Your Mindset 98

Chapter 7: Recoding Your Mindset Operating System 125

Chapter 8: Accept Challenges + Make Mistakes = Robust Mindset 136

Final Words..149

May I ask you for a small favor?.........................151

Full Book Summary...153

Preview of the book "Level-up Your Self Discipline" 165

My Books in Personal Mastery Series 181

Introduction

****

"If you change the way you look at things, the things you look at change."

~ Wayne Dyer

A Short Story: How a Mindset Shift Can Change the Trajectory of Life

There was a middle-aged man in a small town. He had all sorts of bad habits associated with his name. He was a chronic alcoholic; day and night didn't matter to him when it came to drinking. In his drunken state, he was always misbehaving with the people around him. Shouting, abusing, calling names, and any other terrible thing you can think of — he was all that.

All in all, his life was a bit more than a disaster, from a societal standard or any other. With such a state of affairs, doing a day job or working on his own was out of the question. When he ran out of all his saved money, he chose the route of begging

— or if he got a chance, even stealing. He ended up being arrested by the police a number of times for creating a nuisance and committing petty crimes.

Unfortunately, he had two sons in their early teenage years. Sorry, but what else could one call these two children other than unfortunate; negative impressions were getting imprinted on their innocent minds at such an early age.

With the passage of time, the man did not improve; rather, his situation only worsened — deteriorating further with each passing day, week and month. He died after only a few years, leaving behind his two sons.

The elder son was a true follower and started living a life very much like his father's. Drinking, gambling, drugs, etc. — he got into all kinds of negative activities and pursuits. His circle of friends included thieves, smugglers and other sort of criminals, so he was always surrounded with negative associations. In fact, he started exceeding his role model (i.e., his father) and ended up getting arrested by the police and put in jail for some serious criminal offenses.

On the other hand, the younger son, with such a terrible family condition and no financial support, was obviously not in a position to continue his studies. But he didn't want to end up like his father or brother; he had a deep sense of commitment to live a better quality of life. So, he started working in the evenings at burger joints serving tables and was able to manage his school fees out of his meager earnings.

His complete dedication and focus very shortly earned him a good annual scholarship to sponsor his studies. He continued to maintain his focus and kept going on the right track. Eventually, he got a decent job offer to work in a blue-chip company. Not only that, but due to his traits of deep focus and commitment, in only a short period of time, he became part of senior management and was made responsible for operating a specific unit of the organization. Soon his success was creating a ripple effect, his reputation in the industry was spreading, and he was invited for an interview on a TV show.

The TV anchor asked him about his family background, childhood, and growth trajectory and the specific reasons behind his success. He told the whole story of his father — his many wrongdoings and abdicating of all family responsibilities. He also told about his brother following the footsteps of his father and spoiling his own life, when during all those years, this younger son was putting in hard work and building his career. The TV anchor became very curious as to how these two brothers from similar origins had such divergent trajectories in their lives. She wanted to interview the elder brother as well to understand the deeper reasons behind the path he had chosen.

So, the TV crew traveled to the jail to interview the elder son, who was serving a sentence for his crimes. The anchor asked him, "How did you come to end up here, in this shady prison, at this early stage of your life?" The elder son replied with a stony face, "What else could be the fate of a person whose father was a drunken, ill-behaved man, who had done nothing to improve the lives of his children?"

Immediately, the anchor turned the camera to the younger son and questioned him, "And how is it that you've become so successful despite your father being a chronic alcoholic, ill-behaved, and irresponsible man his whole life?"

The younger son replied with a deep sincerity, *"How can a person choose to destroy his life when he has seen first his father wasting his life and then his brother following in his father's very footsteps? I didn't want to waste my life, so I had no choice but to follow a different and better route to design my life."*

Short story, but a grand life message! Two persons facing the same life circumstances had alternate perception of life and prediction of their future entirely on two different extremes.

One thinks that life has presented the circumstances before him and he must live strictly within those circumstances. He thinks there is nothing he can do to change his lot in life, and **considers himself in a victim's position.**

Another person, by contrast, might question whether he is bound to live his life as per these unfavorable circumstances or if he indeed has a choice. Is he bound to live as a victim, or can he **choose to place himself in the driver's seat,** mapping his own course before him — an entirely marvelous way of living a dream life.

This story reminds me of a wonderful quote by Dan Brown, the bestselling author of *The Da Vinci Code*: ***"Sometimes a change of perspective is all it takes to see the light."***

Anyone can see the difference in approach adopted by both sons of the irresponsible father.

The key difference is in their MINDSET – the **manner in which you look at things** that come your way- **your perspective on the people and situation** around you, i.e., **the lens** your eyes see the world through.

This simple personal philosophy, or the way of looking at things, is the single most important factor that makes all the difference as to whether you live an average or mediocre life... or leave a legacy behind.

You can be in any life situation or circumstance — it could be the worst of the worst situation — and, still, with a positive mindset, you can find a calmer version of yourself than you otherwise would.

Okay, now let's get out of the fictional world and

put the spotlight on you.

You might be wondering: how can you get the best out of this story and eventually this book? You might be seeking to know about this mindset thing before you even think of upgrading it.

A one-liner statement, *"Mindset is a way of looking at things in a particular way,"* is simple to *say* intellectually, but it is really difficult to truly implement and get the maximum benefit out of it.

Some Relevant Questions:

You might be thinking about a few relevant and important questions like below:

- How are **our minds different from our mindset**?
- What is so **special about the mindsets of super-achievers**? And how do they acquire them?
- How is it possible to be in such a resourceful state of mind when you are **surrounded by negative people**?
- Is such a growth-oriented mindset only for a limited number of people who are lucky enough to get it as a gift from God, or **can any human being access and attain a resourceful mindset?**

I know those reading this book are precisely the very people who want to enhance their quality of life. I don't know about your personal life situations. You might be struggling to reach even your minimum desired level of success and live a reasonable life, or you could be someone who has already achieved moderate success and wants to reach the next level of his journey.

You could progress to any stage of your life and still find successful people ahead of you, from whom you can learn. I sincerely believe and hope you do as well that the journey of progress never stops. There is always room to grow and more that can be achieved. That's the beauty of this life that makes everyone wake up each morning and start the day with a hope of doing, each day, better than the last.

Attaining any level of growth or progress in life requires a positive and open outlook that triggers initial actions and then further paves the way to an exciting journey. You need to upgrade your mindset to first perceive the outside world, people and situations, the way high-achievers do, before you start to take empowered action towards your most important goals.

And that's what this book is all about – to upgrade, redesign and finally create a whole new mindset that helps you thrive in this world.

What you can get by upgrading your mindset:

- You open up to learning new concepts that expedites your growth at a much faster pace.

- You start to view problems as challenges and opportunities to learn from and grow.

- You become mentally resilient and perseverant to bounce back from failure with more zeal and vigor.

- You start to take more risks and, therefore, increase the rate of your learning by the failures and successes that emanate from the results.

- People start to perceive you as trustworthy person who is deeply motivated to learn, grow and contribute.

- You attract the right quality of people and events in your life, as your behavior and attitude impel people towards you.

- You increase your probability of better career growth. You can get promoted faster or if a business owner, you will take more risks, learn faster and thus earn more.

- As you are willing to learn from every person or situation, you improve the quality of your relations with colleagues, friends and family.

- And the list continues...

What you will learn from this book?

The aim of this book is to radically shift your perspective so you will perceive this world differently.

Although the story in this introduction may be a piece of fiction, in the real-world, we all hear life-changing and empowering stories of people who didn't give up in adverse situations. Rather, they demonstrated how one can turn things around and make the best out of adverse situations, just with a different outlook on life. (In the next chapter, we will see many real-life instances.)

I personally believe that if you're in a position to read this book on an electronic device or you have bought it, you have access to the basic amenities of life like electricity and the internet. So your situation is not as bad as the younger son in the story. I can say with assurance say that if you have a paying job or run your own small business venture, you already are in the top 5% (or maybe 1%) of the population of the world. Some of you might doubt this; and for those readers, I urge you to verify it at www.globalrichlist.com.

After realizing that you are in top 1% of the world population in terms of income or wealth, you'll understand that if the younger son could face adverse conditions (or your real-life heroes) and turn around his life, **you yourself are capable of taking charge of your mindset and, eventually, your destiny.**

I pray to God that no one be forced to suffer the kind of life we saw in the story due to bad parenting. No one should struggle so hard in adversities to live a better life, but at the end of the day, no one can be sure of what life has to offer. Therefore, the best approach is **to see life as a school, teaching us practical lessons by posing challenges and obstacles.**

You can treat this book as a recipe for overcoming life's adversities and problems and turning them into a challenge and adventure, as a pathway to your dreams.

What I want for you is to wake up every morning wondering what life has to offer- not just wondering, but filled with the thrill and excitement of facing any challenges in life.

Just a quick example from my corporate job days. I had the privilege of working with a manager who had the habit of the seeing "goodness" in everything that came his way, even if it was a terrible situation. The only word I heard from him was **'beautiful'** in the face of any challenge.

I really loved that approach as it immediately would bring a smile to my face and I would simply gear up to face the situation head on.

Do you want to see your life as beautiful, whatever color it comes in?

Do you want to welcome life circumstances as they come and make the most out of them?

If yes, then get ready to embark on a wonderful journey.

Here Is What You Are Going To Learn In This Book

We will first of all start to align your self-image and self-talk. Before you conquer the outside wars, you need to win the battle inside your own head.

You can't stay at your physical home; nor can you stay within your mind and thoughts at all times. The universe is created in such a way that you have to go out and meet people and touch other lives or get touched by them. When you have to be around people, then why not design your life in such a way that every touch and connection enhances your quality of life.

We will talk about how to insulate your life from the negative influences of the outside world, and more specifically how to deal with the negative people around us (optional and mandatory negative partners).

Then we will work on designing your everyday life with great habits that support your journey towards building a growth mindset.

Once you have identified and created your own new inside world, mastered quality habits, surrounded yourself with the right set of people, then you will learn how to welcome life's challenges and turn around the quality of your life.

You will embrace mistakes and learn lessons from them. You will persist and persevere and take the necessary lessons this life has to offer.

Okay, enough for an introduction. Now, let's get started.

Introduction Key Takeaways

There can be any worst of worst life situation, but with right mindset to look at the circumstances, one can deal with situations as challenge and design their life. At the same time, with lack of right mindset, one would always feel like a victim of circumstances and out of control of their lives.

Mindset is the **manner in which you look at the things** that come your way- **your perspective of the people and situation** around you- **the lens** you put on your eyes to see the world around.

With an upgraded mindset, you will benefit in all areas of your life, be they financial, relationships, personal growth, social circle or any other aspects of life.

This book will offer you a recipe to **shift your perspective by first designing your inner world and then designing your outer world**, so you can take the challenges head and make the most of it, and ultimately become the captain of your own ship.

Chapter 1: Human Potential is Unknowable but Limitless

****

*"Only those who will risk
going too far can possibly find
out how far one can go."*

~ T.S. Eliot, poet

Let me ask you a simple question. Before embarking on any type of journey in your physical world, do you want to be sure of the destination?

I know it's obvious. Of course everyone wants to.

But here is something interesting when we talk about journey of upgrading our mindsets. The journey of upgrading your mindset doesn't have any endpoint. You wouldn't want to limit yourself by creating a mediocre destination, when you have the possibility of reaching a higher pinnacle. You might not be even aware of it today based on the mindset you have created so far through limited past experiences and the standards of surrounding people.

Instead, the journey of ramping up your mindset is a limitless one. It's only when you embark on this journey and start making some progress that you'll realize on the inside that it is an infinite journey. And putting any false limits or a destination on it will defeat the purpose.

Why would you want to set a limit when you don't know how far you can go?

Therefore, the best approach is keep in mind that your potential is unknowable until you put effort into attaining anything you want. You have endless possibilities that you can't even fathom now based on your current mindset.

Our minds, and to a great extent our bodies, can do stellar things that a layman might term magical or miraculous.

We started this book with a story to convey a particular message, but now we will enter the real world. You're going to read a few real life examples, where humans with their bodies and minds have literally surprised the common man and appear to have super powers.

Let's get started with some real-life instances with the below question.

Can you guess **how much a human being can run in one spurt?**

Before reading further, just try to guess an answer in your mind. In fact Ellen Langer, a professor of psychology at Harvard University and author of a great book, *Mindfulness,* asked this question to her students. Based on their limited knowledge that a marathon is around twenty-six miles, they gave a high number like thirty-two miles or so.

But those who know a bit more about running understand that an ultra-marathon starts at 31.25 miles and goes way longer in different running formats.

Anyways the students were stunned to know how much a human can run. I was shocked to see this and believe you would be too.

There is a tribe in Copper Canyon in Mexico known as the Tarahumara, who can run for 200 miles in one spurt[1].

Out of curiosity, I searched for the longest marathon race and was about to fall off my chair when I read the number. It was astronomical. Sri Chinmoy, an Indian spiritual leader, created a self-transcendence race of 2700 miles in New York in 1996. And adding to the shock, the distance was increased to 3100 miles in the year 1997[2].

This multi-day race is hosted by the Sri Chinmoy Marathon Team and takes place in New York in the United States every year. The course is 3,100 miles (4,989 km) long. It is a race so long that the runners need a haircut during it. They go through 20 pairs of shoes. They run more than two

---

[1] https://www.runnersworld.com/runners-stories/a20954821/born-to-run-secret.s-of-the-tarahumara/

[2] https://www.bbc.com/sport/48702452

marathons a day for almost two months – on five hours of sleep a night.

This race has been described as the "Everest of ultra-running." More than 4,000 have reached the summit of Everest since 1953, but only 43 people have ever completed the Self-Transcendence in around two decades since it started.

This definitely looks like a pinnacle of human body potential. But who knows, if the human body can go this far, it might go further as well. It exemplifies what T.S. Eliot quoted, something worth repeating here: *"Only those who will risk going too far can possibly find out how far one can go."*

This shows that if we don't bind ourselves in false self-limits, our potential is literally limitless.

Let's talk about another story.

It would be an injustice to talk about the vastness of human potential, if we don't cover the story of a **Swedish adventurer Goran Kropp**[3]

In October of 1995, this man started a journey from Stockholm, Sweden, on his bicycle. He rode all the way and reached at the base of Himalayas in April of 1996.

He didn't take an oxygen mask with him, nor did he have the help of any of the sherpas (the local people who know the mountain routes well and

---

[3] This story was captured by Joe De Sena in *Spartan Up*.

accompany the mountaineers). Hence, without an oxygen mask or any help, this brave man reached the summit of Mount Everest on his own. After touching the apex of mountain, he then descended normally, picked up his bike and peddled back to Sweden.

Although this would definitely seem like a life-threatening exercise to anyone, nevertheless Kropp did it. It's crazy, very difficult, but definitely he showed that it was not impossible. This shows how humans can stretch their bodies to such an extent that the common man doesn't think it less than a miracle.

Now let's look at one final famous example of vastness of human potential. Before May 6, 1954, in the sports of running, no one ever believed that humans could run a mile under 4 minutes. It was as if there was limit put on human potential by some unknown force. There wasn't any evidence, but so far no one had ever crossed the **4-minute a mile mark** in the history of athletics.

Then came **Roger Bannister**, a British athlete, who wanted to break this barrier, as he believed that this number was some imaginary limit. People laughed at him when they heard about his crazy dream. But Bannister was so determined that he made a complete mindset shift in his head about achieving the goal of breaking this long and ill-perceived limitation of human capacity.

He visualized his success first in his mind and

then worked towards physically achieving it. He practiced over and over in his mind and envisioned himself breaking that 4-minute a mile barrier. He trained his body with long hours of practice and determination. And finally he broke this human mental limitation.

All the mental and physical hard work paid off. Bannister reached the finish line at the University of Oxford's Iffley road track on May 6, 1954 by setting a record of finishing in 3 minutes and 59.4 seconds.

Don't think that this was just another world record; rather it was the day of busting an age-long myth of putting limits on human potential. And the impact was clearly seen in next few months. Within months of Bannister breaking the 4-minute a mile barrier, more than few dozen athletes broke his record.

That's why someone said it right: ***"If any ONE can do it, ANYONE can do it."***

Bannister's strong determination proved to the world that there are no physical limits, rather they are limits set by humans only in their minds. That's why the saying goes.

The above stories indicate how humans can do seemingly magical things with their bodies. In fact, the United States Navy's Sea, Air and Land Teams, commonly known as Navy SEALs, are trained through one tough rule to get the maximum out of their physical potential. They call it the 40% Rule.

The 40% Rule of Human Potential

Navy SEALs are taught in their tough training that whenever they feel the first sign of fatigue, it doesn't mean that they are really got tired and can stop. They are told that when they get the first inkling of fatigue or tiredness, they have just used only 40% of their physical capacity and are still left with 60% more.

Don't think that this 40% rule is merely a bold statement, rather it is **backed up by psychological research.** Timothy Noakes[4], a professor at University of Cape Town, dived deep into how long a person could still continue in his physical adventures, despite getting a signal from the mind to stop and not go any further.

He decided to explore a lesser-known theory proposed by the Nobel Prize winner physiologist, Archibald Hill, that **exercise fatigue may not be caused by muscle failure, but by an overprotective monitor in the brain that wants us to avoid exhaustion.** As per the theory, when the body is working hard and pushing the heart to demand more from it, this monitor in the brain activates the body to slow things down. Noakes was intrigued to find, however, that **physical exhaustion is in fact a trick played by the mind on the body.** The capacity of the body is much greater.

---

[4] http://bjsm.bmj.com/content/39/2/120.short

Noakes began to review the evidence of levels of physical exertion of endurance athletes under extreme conditions. **In the study, he didn't find any evidence of physiological failure within the muscles. It was rather the brain telling them to stop**. This is because the brain was sensing an increased heart rate and rapidly decreasing supply of energy and therefore gave the message to the body to stop. In short, the brain started to impart an overwhelming feeling of fatigue, but it had nothing to do with muscles capacity to keep working. **Noakes concluded that perceived fatigue should no longer be considered a physical event, but rather a sensation or emotion.**

Therefore, all high-performing athletes know that the first wave of fatigue is not the real physical limit of the body. They know that with enough motivation, they can transcend this limit.

In all these examples, we talked about the human body's capabilities, which from a normal human's perspective are not less than an extraordinary achievement. Some people might think such achievers are gifted with some sort of supernatural powers.

Still it is all about human body, which, of course, is governed by the limitations of time and space.

Now let's look at some examples that demonstrate the limitless potential of the human mind and its thinking capabilities.

Yes, humans have proven the limitless potential of the mind in countless cases, extending its reach far beyond the limitations of the physical body, time and space.

Vastness of Human Thinking Potential

Look at this man, who is not restricting himself to innovation related to Planet Earth. He is on a mission to make humans as multi-planetary species. He is thinking and taking actions toward setting up a colony of a million people on the planet Mars by 2024.[5] You guessed it: I'm talking about **Elon Musk**, the founder and CEO of SpaceX and Tesla Motors.

He also made a bold proposition recently, stating that in next decade or so he wants to make it possible to travel to any corner of the world in just one hour. How? Check out this YouTube video: *Elon Musk: Anywhere in the World in Less Than One Hour*.[6]

While a normal person might not able to run through his normal day-to-day work tasks to pay his bills, or another might be confused about life and what action to take next, Musk, on the other hand, is thinking *so hugely* that every other thought seems to be dwarfed by comparison, doesn't it?

---

[5] http://www.businessinsider.in/Elon-Musk-has-published-an-outline-of-his-audacious-plan-to-colonize-Mars-with-a-million-people/articleshow/59166030.cms
[6] https://www.youtube.com/watch?v=aMmka9cVFWc

Whether and when the above will happen, time will tell, but thinking with such a gigantic futuristic outlook shows that there can't be any boundaries set on human thinking potential.

For a moment, imagine some of your ancestors from the 19th century visiting the planet now (of course, with their old memory of that time), and they see you flying in the air, doing live video conversions with a person sitting thousands of miles away, and witness many more innovations. They will not treat you less than some kind of wizard.

Today, a small robot (with artificial intelligence) can do so many tasks for you from selecting music, switching lights on or off or making calls – think about Alexa from Amazon.

Hundreds of people including Ashton Kutcher, Leonardo DiCaprio, and Justin Bieber already have placed a hefty deposit for space travel with Unity Spacecraft, a Richard Branson's space travel initiative.

Definitely, broader thinking of modern man would be beyond the imagination of our ancestors and they would definitely be stunned to see all this seemingly miraculous technological development. Similarly, you and I can't even fathom what's going to happen in next 50 or 100 years.

I read somewhere that the amount of data put on the internet from the moment it was created since the start of civilization and up to year 2003 is now created and uploaded in a matter of just days. It is estimated that sum total of data stored by online storage companies like Google, Amazon, Microsoft and Facebook is at least 1,200 petabytes. If you are non-techie like me, one petabyte is equal to 1.2 million terabytes (one terabyte is 1,000 gigabytes). That's really a huge amount of data, and all the information has been collectively created by only the human mind.

Can you see the vastness of human thinking?

It is not just talent, a skillset or any other favorable circumstance that govern success. They do matter, of course, but only if such a talent or skillset are used to think at higher realms to solve the bigger challenges of life and the world in general.

In my personal experience, I have seen people, for example, with three Master's degrees simply sitting in a government-run organizations acting as nothing more than glorified file clerks. You might recall a few names of several highly-qualified or skilled people who, despite great attributes, have not been able to live life up to their true potential.

Please don't take me wrong — I'm not in any manner making fun of such people for their multiple degrees. The point I'm trying to put across is that even though such people are at the height of their skillset and yet they have only reached to such a level which they could only *think* of, through their mindset.

The moot point here is if such people are happy doing what they do, then it's totally fine, because everyone has a different definition of success or fulfilment. But if someone with such a high skillset struggles to lead a better life and considers himself or herself as a victim of circumstances, then, it is nothing but a *mindset* problem.

Let's look at a few more real-life examples.

Richard Branson, a British business magnate, operates more than four hundred businesses under the brand, Virgin Group, which ranges from music records and media to telecom, airlines, commercial space-lines, and more. He also owns his own private island paradise, Necker Island, where he spends his time relaxing, rejuvenating, and running the business.

Do you think he has more than 24 hours in a day available to him? Obviously not! Everyone has just 24 hours in a day. No one is privileged to have even 1 minute more than that. And out of those 24 hours, sleeping and other usual routine affairs can easily take away 8–10 hours, so effectively you are left with just 14–16 hours at the max during which to work.

Is he super-qualified or in possession of any specific training or skillset?

Again, no!

Rather, he dropped out of school at the age of 16. Then, from the age of 20, he has been setting up flourishing businesses decade after decade.

There is a famous story behind Virgin Airlines – how it started from looking at some problem as a challenge and taking action based on inspiration.

It's around 1970's that Branson got stuck at an airport in United States, as the flight to his destination got cancelled and the next available one was available only on the next day. Obviously, people around him were complaining about missing an important meeting or not being able to reach some family function or other important event. Branson was sitting amongst them, but he took a very different action.

He was mindful of the importance of his upcoming meeting, so he took solid action immediately. He called up and hired a chartered plane, despite it being a very costly affair at that point of time in his career. Then he asked his fellow stranded travelers if anyone wanted to board his private plane at a significantly higher price than the regular ticket price. Most chose to pay extra, and Branson was able to recover his cost of chartered plane and even made some money too.

This inspired him to set up Virgin Atlantic Airlines. His famous quote is: *"Take action before you are ready"*

What does Branson have compared to other

people who barely scrape by and are unable to finish even their individual daily task lists? It's all about the way he thinks and operates. People like Branson have nurtured a mindset that focuses on the *possibilities* in life and not on the obstacles.

Now let's talk about Colonel Sanders whose story tells us not only about mindset but about how to persevere despite failure after failure.

Colonel Sanders had many reasons to argue that success is not for everyone. He had been quite a failure in dozens of areas for most of his working life until his late fifties. At that point, his latest business venture became selling chicken dishes from a service station and serving food to travelers. Well, his chicken was so good that before long, people started coming in more for the chicken than the gas!

Finally, Sanders' "secret recipe" was coined "Kentucky Fried Chicken" by a franchisee. It became a tremendous hit and the rest is history. Isn't it amazing how the man persisted long enough to taste success at the age of 65, when most retire, and build a global empire out of a fried chicken business?

This story is inspirational because it is an example of **how the right mindset combined with perseverance and dedication can create success, regardless of age.**

But the most important element, which comes first, is maintaining the right level of mindset.

Despite his many failures, having the right mindset for growth was something that propelled and fueled Sanders to keep going so long.

On the one hand, history is full of child prodigies who succeeded pretty fast in life, but we also know people who tasted success only in their much later years. You will find people like Mark Zuckerberg turning a billionaire in his twenties and on the other hand, are people like Colonel Sanders, who succeeded with KFC in his sixties.

The point in this entire chapter is that human potential is limitless from a mental or physical perspective. **The future is unknown, and there will always endless possibilities for anyone who keeps his or her mind open and is willing to learn and explore more.**

Tony Robbins one said aptly, "Success leaves clues."

You can see a common trait in all high achievers or those who have surprised the world with their physical or mental achievements, because they perceive life differently than the crowd. They have a different outlook and take on life's challenges. In short, they have a different mindset.

Our job is to find those clues left by these legends, understand them deeply, and take massive action to attract success in our lives too.

Knowing our potential is limitless and unknowable until you go so far, let's now start to get deeper into the human mindset before we start to learn effective ways to level it up.

I'll see you in the next chapter.

Chapter 1 Key Takeaways

Humans have always demonstrated tremendous potential in terms of their physical capability as well as thinking ability.

Physically, human can run hundreds of miles in one spurt, climb Mount Everest without any support or break any myth about the human's body's false limits.

In terms of **thinking,** the vastness of human potential is beyond the imagination. People like Elon Musk are trying to make space travel for humans possible. There are plenty of examples of people who have succeeded wildly despite adverse life situations by keeping a positive mindset.

The examples you read in this chapter exemplify the quote by T.S. Eliot, **"Only those who will risk going too far can possibly find out how far one can go."**

The future is unknown and there will always be endless possibilities for anyone who develops the right mindset and is willing to learn and explore.

Chapter 2: Do You Know Your Mindset?

****

"A man cannot directly choose his circumstances, but he can choose his thoughts, and so indirectly, yet surely, shape his circumstances."

~James Allen

The word "mindset" starts with "mind". Mindset is a way of thinking and perceiving something in a particular way that happens only through the mind. Then let's first briefly understand about the human physical brain, and the invisible mind, before we talk about mindset in greater detail.

Understanding Your Brain and Mind

Let's take the analogy of a computer to understand the human brain and mind. A computer requires hardware [screen monitor, CPU (Central Processing Unit) box, keyboard, mouse, etc.] to operate and trigger its functions. But the hardware part needs software [Windows or Mac operating software (OS)] to make it run. Without software, hardware is useless, and without hardware, software cannot be installed.

Your brain is like the hardware and your mind is

like its software.

Your brain is a tangible physical organ in the body. With the brain, you coordinate your moves, various physiological processes and day-to-day activities, and transmit impulses.

The human brain is a complex bundle of neural pathways, with countless neurons connecting/charging each other at all times. Neuroscience has already found that the human brain has more than a hundred billion neurons. And each neuron can have approximately ten thousand connections with other neurons known as synapses, which makes the human brain a vastly complex network.

If we imagine all the stars in the Milky Way galaxy, there are more connections in our brains than all those stars combined. And what is even more amazing is that no two brains are exactly alike. If you physically observe the person next to you and note all the physical differences — the shape of your noses, the color of your eyes, your heights, etc. — there are way more differences between the two brains than all of these superficial physical differences. So, our brains make us uniquely *us*.

Let's now talk about **mind**.

You use your mind to think. The mind is the manifestation of thought, perception, emotion, determination, memory and imagination — that all take place within the brain. **The *mind* is**

often used to refer specifically to the thought processes of reasoning. The mind is awareness of the consciousness we know, the ability to control what we do, and to know what we are doing and why. It is the ability to understand.

Lower animals are able to only *interpret* their environments on a basic level, but they do not *understand* them, whereas humans can understand what happens around them — even if they don't find any scientific reasoning for it — and can therefore adapt.

The *mind* has made humans capable of solving complex logical problems — which differentiates us from the other lesser living beings. Logic makes us understand that things are not as they appear. Our ability to analyze situations makes it possible to develop solutions to problems and leads us toward practical solutions.

With this basic understanding about the human brain and mind, it is necessary to know the underlying tangible and intangible ingredients, so let's now go on to understand the concept of mindset in greater detail.

Mindset – An Approach of Your Mind

Mindset is a particular way of thinking about the circumstances, events or people based on your own unique position or perspective.

A mindset is quite literally a setting of the mind--

a lens or frame of mind through which we view the world and simplify the infinite number of potential interpretations at any given moment. Now, the ability to simplify our world through our mindsets is a natural part of being human.

Therefore, while *mind* is nothing but a combination of thoughts and perceptions in general, *mindset* is a particular attitude toward actions and beliefs.

With the help of our brains and minds, we can survive in this world as human beings by keeping ourselves safe from danger and taking the necessary actions required to go through the journey of life. But it is the *mindset* that determines whether we are able to live a life of grand success or mega failure.

It is a specific type of mindset — or the way we look at things in a particular fashion — that is the sole determinant of whether we get into a resourceful state and make positive decisions and actions or whether we choose to hide ourselves in a cave, so to speak, and do nothing.

Charles R. Swindoll rightly said, *"Life is 10% what happens to you and 90% how you react to it."*

Once the mindset of looking at your circumstances changes for the positive, any goal is achievable. Learning any skillset is important, but skills or tactics come secondary after mindset. Because once again, as Tony Robbins said, *"Success in life is 80% psychology and 20%*

mechanics."

Psychology means the human mindset and mechanics refer to skillsets. We talked in the previous chapter how people with a lack of education or skillset, but with right mindset, can learn everything they needed to become ultra-successful in their lives.

2 Types of Mindset

According to Carol Dweck, a psychology researcher at Stanford University, there are two types of mindsets: **a fixed mindset and a growth mindset.**

The terms, *fixed* and *growth,* give some indication as to what they are. But let's understand a bit of detail about what the two mindset are and how people with specific mindsets behave differently.

In a **fixed mindset**, people believe their **intelligence or mental abilities are fixed traits** and therefore cannot change. These people strongly believe that their intelligence and talents are already carved in stone, so they don't make any effort to develop and improve them.

They also believe that talent alone leads to success and that significant effort is thus not required. A fixed-mindset person thinks that if something is difficult and he is required to put some effort into it, it means that he does not have the right talent or capability. In their words, having to put effort into something means they don't have what it takes, so why even try.

Alternatively, in a **growth mindset**, people have the underlying belief that **their learning and intelligence can grow with time and experience**. When people with such a mindset believe they can get smarter, they realize that effort has an effect on their success, so they put in extra time, leading to higher achievement.

Dweck introduced these ideas and wrote a book to describe each mindset in more detail. She goes on to state that when students have a fixed mindset, **they believe that their basic abilities, intelligence and talents are fixed traits**. They think that they are born with a certain amount and that's all they have got. The goal for people with a fixed mindset is always to look smart, because they believe they were born with that ability. These people have a fear of looking dumb because they do not believe they can redeem themselves once others look at them as being unintelligent.

In a growth mindset, however, **students believe their talents and abilities can be developed through effort, learning and persistence**. Their basic abilities are simply a starting point for their true potential. They don't believe everyone is the same, but they hold onto the idea that everyone can become smarter if they try.

A case study was conducted at the University of Hong Kong where the curriculum was to be substantially delivered in English such that all the lectures in the syllabus were in English. The students were asked if they wanted some lessons in learning the English language.

There were two kinds of answers: the students with a fixed mindset stated that they had a fixed amount of intelligence and couldn't change much, so they were not forthcoming about learning English language. But the students with a growth mindset were willing to learn English because they believed that anyone can substantially change how intelligent they are.

Dweck explained the concept of a growth-mindset in her book. *Mindset: The New Psychology of Success*. She states:

Why waste time proving over and over how great you are, when you could be getting better? Why hide deficiencies instead of overcoming them? Why look for friends or partners who will just shore up your self-esteem instead of ones who will also challenge you to grow? And why seek out the tried and true, instead of experiences that will stretch you? **The passion for stretching yourself and sticking to it, even (or especially) when it's not going well, is the hallmark of the growth mindset.** This is the mindset that allows people to thrive during some of the most challenging times in their lives.

A Real-life Growth Mindset Story

Let's look into a real-life story of a growth mindset, which proves that any new learning, and success from it, is quite possible if you have that mindset. This story is a clear demonstration of the adoption of the ***growth mindset***.

Joshua Waitzkin, an American chess player, was a child prodigy. At the very young age of six, he started playing chess. By the age eleven, he and one other child were the only two children to come to a draw against World Champion, Garry Kasparov, in an exhibition game where Kasparov played simultaneously against 59 youngsters. Then two years later, he earned the title of National Master, and at age 16 became an International Master.[7]

He is an eight-time National Chess Champion and the subject of the book and movie, *Searching for Bobby Fischer*. At eighteen, he published his first book, *Josh Waitzkin's Attacking Chess*. Since the age of twenty, Waitzkin has developed and been a spokesperson for the Josh Waitzkin Academy, for *Chessmaster*, the largest computer chess program in the world.

But you will be surprised to look at his life trajectory and the major career shifts he made. His decisions show a perfect example of carrying a growth mindset. He was such a believer in learning that he chose as his next passion a sport that was altogether different from the one he had

---

[7] https://en.wikipedia.org/wiki/Joshua_Waitzkin

earlier mastered.

At the pinnacle of his career, based on a highly cognitive skill (chess), he chose now to learn and master an extreme physical skill-based sport – martial arts. In his next book, *The Art of Learning: An Inner Journey to Optimal Performance*, he explains the reason for choosing an altogether different sport. He states that he wanted to test his potential as a human being. He wanted to validate his belief that that human mind can learn and master anything.

Giving the example of chess, he states that **winning every next game, of a level superior to the last, itself proves that the mind has immense potential to learn and grow to any extent**. The power of mindset can lead a man to think beyond his imagination. With this strong belief, he chose to take on a fresh and new challenge — going from a mental game to a sport requiring great physical strength and alertness.

And very soon, he proved his mastery in martial arts. Josh Waitzkin is a martial arts champion and holds a combined twenty-one National Championship titles in addition to several World Championship titles.[8]

You see here two entirely dissimilar endeavors and how he was able to achieve mastery in both all

---

[8] https://www.amazon.com/Josh-Waitzkin/e/B001IGT18M/ref=ntt_dp_epwbk_0

through the power of the growth mindset.

Why You Should Not Label Your Child

Note that labeling someone as smart doesn't help, because labeling any child as dumb or smart makes them think like that, so they tend to take action accordingly. Once you label them as smart kids and then if the competition fails them, they can't prove they are smart and it adversely impacts their self-image.

What should you do instead?

Instead of labelling, the child should be told that if she works harder and smarter, she will get good results. **Instead of labeling the person as a particular type, promote the behavior that gets results.**

In experiments with school children, Dweck found a surprising result. Praising children's talent or intelligence ruins their motivation and lowers their academic performance. Of course, praising their talent will make them happy and proud, but only for a short while.

But as soon as they face a challenge or setback, their confidence fades away, because if success is a sign that they are smart, failure should mean they lack talent and proves them dumb (**fixed mindset**). Therefore, we should avoid praising our children's talent or intelligence and, instead, praise them for their diligence, effort and conscientiousness (**growth mindset**).

Now let's understand these two types of mindset from a different perspective. After all, we understand that mindset is nothing but looking at things from a particular perspective. So why not look at the very concept of mindset from a different angle.

Big Thinking vs. Small Thinking

Michael Port, in his great book, *The Think Big Manifesto*, explains how one should choose every moment between Thinking Big and Thinking Small. He suggests that when choosing between the two options, one must continuously gauge whether they are thinking big or thinking small.

Let's try to understand this by way of an example.

If you are a student, corporate worker or a self-employed solopreneur -- whatever you do for a living -- you always have two types of thoughts running through your head, one that focuses on favorable and long-term results, and another that stops you and forces you to stay safe and comfortable.

Assuming you are a student preparing for a tough examination or your big goal is to get admission to a reputed educational institution, then two types of thoughts will be competing in your mind:

Small Thinking

- This competition is too big for me — there's no way I can get into such a prestigious school.
- I am not that smart.
- I don't have any significant past experience that shows evidence of me being able to succeed at this.
- Precisely who am *I* to be succeeding in this exam?
- People will make fun of me or I will look stupid if I fail.

Big Thinking

- If I work hard, then I can learn — and by practice, I can master anything.
- I am just as worthy as anyone else to succeed in this goal.
- Everyone does everything for the first time before succeeding. So if *they* can crack it, *I* can too. I can follow in their footsteps and find success as well.
- Even if I fail, I will learn something new in the process. Not even trying will most certainly get me absolutely nowhere. So, better to try something new.

To put it simply, small thinking starts with limiting beliefs and therefore restricts you from taking action. Therefore you get mediocre or no results. But thinking big opens you up to explore, learn, take action, and then results are bound to follow sooner or later.

Everyone has different life situations and circumstances and, accordingly, everyone has to make different life choices. Take your own current goals or projects — whatever is in front of you— and you have to choose between big thinking and small thinking.

Let's use the **analogy of a big thought being a divine angel and a small thought as a little devil each sitting on one of your shoulders.** Don't just read, but visualize for a moment that both are sitting on each shoulder. While writing this, I'm visualizing that a divine angel is sitting on my right shoulder talking to and encouraging my imaginative brain, and the little devil sitting on the left shoulder is prompting my inner critic.

Of course, you'll hear both voices, but *you* have the choice to implement *your* decision. The more you listen and act upon the advice of your divine angel, the sooner you will start seeing better results.

Those results may be small and slow at first, but they will be incremental. But, in this way, you will strengthen the voice; it will become much louder and clearer over time and, simultaneously, it will calm down your inner little monster.

Mindset Assessment Quiz Online

I found this quick quiz online that can help you gauge where you stand on the mindset scale. It's just a 20 multiple-choice question that will take just 5 minutes of your time. You'll get to see your mindset score and type.

Click this short link to take this quiz: https://www.positivityguides.net/test-your-mindset-quiz/

I tested myself and found that I am more inclined towards a growth mindset, because I love taking challenges, learning and exploring new things, seeing where my curiosities will lead me.

Test yourself to see where you are on the mindset scale.

I also found one questionnaire published by Carol Dweck named, Dweck Mindset Instrument (DMI) that gives you 16 different questions to check your beliefs about learning, failure, taking challenges, growth, etc. Unfortunately this online resource doesn't give you a score card, so I was wondering whether I should put it in this book or not. But I did put it here, so you can at least have a look at the questions asked by a mindset researcher and expert.

Here is the link for DMI: https://osf.io/pjwgs/. This will at least help you listen to your own beliefs and approaches to different kinds of life situations.

Chapter 2 Key Takeaways

Your brain and mind can be compared to computer hardware (like the CPU, monitor screen, keyboard, etc.) and software (like Windows or iOS, Microsoft Office, etc.), respectively.

The brain is your physical hardware with billions of neurons, responsible for coordinating your moves, various physiological processes, and day-to-day activities.

The mind is the manifestation of thought, perception, emotion, determination, memory and imagination — that all take place within the brain.

Mindset is a particular way of thinking about circumstances, events or people based on your own unique position or perspective. It's a setting of the mind, a lens or frame of mind through which we view the world.

Therefore, while *mind* is a combination of thoughts and perceptions in general, *mindset* is a particular attitude toward actions and beliefs.

There are two types of mindsets:

Fixed mindset: people with this mindset believe their intelligence or mental abilities are fixed traits and therefore cannot be changed. Failure for them means they don't have what it takes to succeed. Putting effort into something means wasting time.

Growth mindset: people with a growth mindset have an underlying belief that their learning and intelligence can grow with time and experience. Failure means the opportunity to learn and grow and putting in effort means they can master any skill they want.

You **shouldn't label your child as smart and dumb**, as it makes him or her behave according to the label. Instead of labeling in a particular way, tell the child about the behavior that will make him or her achieve success in life.

Listen to your divine angel (big thinking) and don't pay attention to your little devil (small thinking) to strengthen growth mindset. It will help you take action, learn and grow to become the best version of yourself.

You can test your mindset type on a scale by answering the simple questionnaire given in the chapter.

Chapter 3: Use Neuroplasticity- 5 Pillars to Redesign Your Mindset

****

"You're in charge of your mind. You can help it grow by using it in the right way."

~Carol Dweck

Unfortunately, we live in a world that cherishes "natural" talent and believes we're either BORN a genius or we've got no hope.

But, that's just not true. If you look at the history of legends born on this planet, there are more than enough examples to bust this myth.

In fact, most of the geniuses we know today didn't have any an indication in their childhood of rising to future greatness. They were not granted some magical brain; rather, they might have been simply considered average or normal at the time.

- **Ben Hogan**, one of the greatest golfer of all time was completely uncoordinated and graceless as a child.

- Legends like **Mohammad Ali** and **Michael Jorden** faced very challenging times in their childhoods and were ridiculed by people.

- **Einstein**'s mother was told by his school principal that her son wouldn't amount to much in his life.

- **Walt Disney** was told that he simply lacked imagination.

- Did you know that **Darwin and Tolstoy** were just ordinary kids?

While we looked at a child prodigy like Joshua Waitzkin in the previous chapter, there are way more examples in history where geniuses were not born but were made by sheer persistence and a positive outlook towards life.

Michael Jordan is famous for embracing failure time and time again until he reached success. He has a famous quote:

> *"I've missed more than 9,000 shots in my career. I've lost almost 300 games. Twenty-six times, I've been trusted to take the game winning shot and missed. I've failed over and over and over again in my life. And that is why I succeed."*

In fact, the success stories of all these people show what Michael Gelb, the author of *Think Like Leonardo da Vinci*, rightly said, **"Genius are made not born."**

There has been a lot of debate in the past as to whether we can change our mindsets. Is change possible or are we slaves to the specific type we possess?

Unfortunately, a few decades ago, the common understanding was that human intelligence is limited; people believed that the human mind has a fixed capacity from birth, and it can't be changed any further.

But thanks to research conducted in the field of neuroscience and human psychology, we now have the concept of neuroplasticity. The good news is that **science has concluded that there is no such thing such as a fixed or only-once wired mind**. Rather, it has the potential to keep changing during one's lifetime, thanks to an awareness of the concept of neuroplasticity.

Neuroplasticity is the ability of your brain to reorganize itself, both physically and functionally, throughout your life due to changes in one's environment, behavior, thinking and emotions. With the recent capability to visually "see" into the brain with the help of the fMRI (functional magnetic resonance imagining), science has confirmed its **incredible morphing ability** beyond any doubt.

Norman Doidge explains the concept of our brain's elasticity in his book, *The Brain That Changes Itself: Stories of Personal Triumph from the Frontiers of Brain Science* below: "The brain is not an inanimate vessel that we fill; rather it is more like a living creature with an appetite, **one that can grow and change itself with proper nourishment and exercise.**"

The good news is that your brain makes physical changes based on the repetitive things you do and the experiences you have. The bad news is that your brain makes physical changes based on the repetitive things you do and the experiences you have. Therefore, this morphing capability of your brain, known as neuroplasticity, works both for and against you.

The resourceful characteristic of neuroplasticity, which can make your brain amazingly resilient, also makes it very vulnerable to both outside and internal (usually unconscious) influences.

Norman Doidge calls this the ***plastic paradox.*** Think about it. Your brain actually wires itself and forms neuronal connections based on what you do over and over in your life. Lying on your couch for hours in front of the TV with a king-sized burger and fries, having a sugar fix, sipping soda, fixing a cocktail to unwind after work, or smoking cigarettes. Whether you want to call them bad habits or addictions, these activities literally become wired into your brain.

Lara Boyd, a brain researcher at University of British Columbia stated[9] that in order to support

---

[9] https://www.youtube.com/watch?v=LNHBMFCzznE

new learning, our brains can change based on the concept of neuroplasticity at three specific levels:

1. **Changes at the brain's chemical level**: At this level, the brain functions by transferring chemical signals between brain cells, known as neurons, which triggers a series of actions and reactions. In order to support new learning, your brain can increase the amount and concentrations of these chemical signalings taking place between neurons. Because this kind of change can happen rapidly, it supports short-term memory or the short-term improvement in the performance of a motor skill.

2. **Changes at the brain's structure level**: The second way that the brain can change to support learning is by *altering its structure*. During learning, the brain changes the connections between neurons. Here the physical structure of the brain is actually changing so it takes a bit more time. These changes are related to long-term memory and long-term improvement in a motor skill.

3. **Changes at the brain's functional level**: The last way that your brain can change to support learning is by *altering its function*. As you use a brain region, it becomes more and more excitable and easy to use again. And as your brain has areas that increase excitability, the brain shifts how and when they are activated. With learning, we see that whole

networks of brain activity are shifting and changing.

How Brain's Neuroplasticity Can Grow Your Brain (A real-life story)

The miraculous life story of a little girl named Cameron Mott[10], from North Carolina, proves the vast potential of neuroplasticity on our brain's abilities. Just after her third birthday, Cameron started having violent seizures. They became worse, and eventually she lost her ability to speak. Doctors diagnosed her with something called Rasmussen's encephalitis, a rare inflammatory neurological disease, and the only real treatment was hemispherectomy—cutting out half of her brain.

The impact of this surgery was to be very catastrophic for this girl because one half of your brain controls and is responsible for movement and sensation in the other half of your body, i.e., the left hemisphere controls the right side of your entire body's function, and vice versa. This surgery would immediately leave Cameron hemiplegic, meaning suffering from paralysis on one side of the body.

But to everyone's utmost surprise, just four weeks post-operation, she walked out of the hospital.

---

[10] https://www.theconfidentteacher.com/2017/09/a-new-school-year-and-a-new-start/

And after few months of difficult rehabilitation, she returned to good health and was again going to school, participating in school activities, and living a life of miraculous normality. She was free from seizures after the surgery, and despite having half of her brain removed, she was able to live a normal life.

How could 50% of the brain work almost like 100% for Cameron?

It happened because the remaining part of Cameron's brain sensed the massive loss of neural tissue and it physically rewired and reorganized itself to take over everything that the other half had previously handled. This proves the vast ability of the brain to change itself—to rewire.

Science has shown that neuroplastic changes happen throughout our entire lives, regardless of age or any other factor. Radical improvements in cognitive function—how we learn, think, perceive, and remember—are possible even in the elderly. **Your brain makes physical changes based on the repetitive things you do and the experiences you have**.

This validates that the below quote by Jim Rohn has some scientific backing. He stated: *"You are the average of the five people you spend the most time with."*

The science-based research and real-life stories in the book prove that you are not stuck with your mind in whatever way it gets formed over a period of time. You have the capability to change your mindset -- the way you look and perceive different things in your life -- at any stage and age.

5 Pillars to Design a Robust Mindset

All the further chapters in this book are all about the *solution* part of the equation. You are going to learn how to effectively implement the concept of neuroplasticity by changing your behavior, actions and environment in order to design a new set of neural pathways that can surely lead to a life of happiness, fulfillment and success.

If you have been reading personal development books for some time, these concepts may not be new to you. You might already know them, but the key problem is that most people don't implement the knowledge and keep looking for new information, because this gives hope that you might get a shortcut to make a quick shift.

Moreover, one of the key reasons for not implementing new knowledge by most people is that most of the time, the information is bit scattered, and it lacks a structure. You and I know that this is already an information overload age: we don't need more and new information. Your mind wants some structure or a roadmap to arrive at a destination without too much information; precisely, you need a recipe to design your mindset.

Therefore, the next sections of this book are designed to offer a structured path to help you achieve the objective of redesigning your mind.

Everything starts inside us before it takes shape in outside words. Therefore, we will start with working on our self-image and self-talk. Then we will work on redesigning our environment in terms of dealing with people. To bring consistency and automaticity, so that we don't keep drifting to past behaviors, you'll learn some effective routines that fit into your daily schedule. A good life is nothing but a combination of days intentionally lived well.

Following this, we will work on feeding our brain, just like upgrading the software at frequent intervals, so it adapts itself to deal with the latest viruses or bugs. As they rightly say, if you are not moving ahead, you're going backwards.

And last but not the least, as we all know, despite our best intentions and sincerely following the right practices, life at times will throw you challenges and adversities that can either distract or disrupt you. So you will learn how to train your mind to become ready to handle any such adversity and thus become a resilient mindset.

To do this, there are five pillars to design a robust mindset that we will learn in the rest of this book:

1. **Self-image and self-talk** (inner mastery)

2. Redesigning your **surrounding environment**

3. Automating a mindset upgrade by **effective daily routines**
4. **Recoding** a new mindset operating system
5. **Toughening your mindset** to become resilient

Now with this precise structure to upgrade your mind, let's jump straight into the action.

Chapter 3 Key Takeaways

Modern history is filled with examples of legends, who despite their unfavorable childhoods or even less than average beginnings, turn out to disrupt the world with their genius.

Therefore, the concept of "born genius or else no hope" is a myth. Instead, in the words of Michael Gelb, *"Geniuses are made not born."*

Research and the invention of brain imaging technologies like the fMRI have proven the incredible morphing abilities of the brain. The concept of neuroplasticity proves the **ability of your brain to reorganize itself, both physically and functionally, throughout your life due to changes in your environment, behavior, thinking and emotions**.

As per Lara Boyd, you can change your brain at the chemical, structural and functional level. The real-life incident in the chapter shows how 50% of your brain can handle 100% of your brain activities, thanks to the reorganizing abilities our brain.

Your brain makes physical changes based on the repetitive things you do and the experiences you have. Therefore, you need to do specific activities or design new behavior to change your mindset.

The following are the **5 pillars to build a robust mindset** to upgrade your mindset:

1. **Self-image and self-talk** (inner mastery)
2. Redesigning your **surrounding environment**
3. Automating a mindset upgrade by **effective daily routines**
4. **Recoding a** new mindset operating system.
5. **Toughening your mindset** to become resilient

Chapter 4: Building Self Image and Re-narrating Self-Talk

****

"If I have the belief that I can do it, I shall surely acquire the capacity to do it even if I may not have it at the beginning."

~Gandhi

Okay, let's shift the gears and start to learn the strategies to upgrade our mindset.

The objective of the introduction and previous few chapters was to help you understand the basic concepts of mindset and give you a glimpse of the vastness of human potential. It was necessary because, without the support of evidence from neuroscience, your rational mind may simply ignore the concept of mindset, considering it some woo-woo or mystical thing. But now with neuroscience-based research, it has been proven that anyone can change their mindset and start to view life differently, if they are committed to learn and implement new behavior.

With this groundwork in place, the natural progression of this book is to understand the steps and practical ways to re-design your mindset.

So, let's get going, starting with the **concept of self-image.**

While the concept of mindset is all about your outlook and approach to things, if we go granular and deeper (and we have to), the first thing to start with is to change and upgrade our self-image, or the way we think about ourselves.

Our self-image plays a vital role in how we approach any activity and, therefore, our behavior and performance. And there is good news. We can change our self-image to improve our performance. We will get to how to change one's self-image, but before that, let's understand more about self-image.

There is a broader term known as **self-concept** and one of its subsets is self-image. Carl Rogers, an American psychologist, believed that the self-concept has three components:

1. **Self-image:** the view you have of yourself.
2. **Self-esteem or self-worth**: how much value you place on yourself
3. **Ideal self:** what you wish you were really like

How to ascertain your self-image

In 1954, Manfred Kuhn, a social psychologist, developed a tool known as ***The Twenty Statements Test (TST)***[11] that he used to investigate further into the self-image. He would ask people to answer the question "Who am I?" in 20 different ways and in the process, he realized that the responses could be divided into two major groups: (1) ***social roles*** (external or objective aspects of oneself such as son, teacher, or friend) and (2) ***personality traits*** (internal or affective aspects of oneself such as sympathetic, impatient, or humorous).

The list of answers to the question "Who Am I?" includes examples of each of the following four types of responses:

1. **Physical description**: I'm tall, have blue eyes, etc.

2. **Social roles:** We are all social beings and our behavior is shaped to some extent by the roles we play. Such roles as being a student, housewife, or member of any sports team not only help others to recognize us, but at the same time, these roles help us know what is expected of us in various situations.

---

[11] http://psychology.wikia.com/wiki/Twenty_Statements_Test

3. **Personal traits:** This is another dimension of our self-description. You might give personal traits like "I'm impulsive...I'm generous...I tend to worry a lot."

4. **Existential statements** (abstract ones): These can range from "I'm a child of the universe" and "I'm a human being" to "I'm a spiritual being"...etc.

Depending upon your age, social connections, relationships and behaviors, your answers to these questions will vary.

You will realize that answering them will help you see your self-image in a broader sense – and that realization itself makes you understand why you perform a particular task in your own way or avoid doing it.

For example, assume your self-image whispers in your head, "I am shy guy." Now, imagine your behavior if you were to attend a crowded party. Your first thought would be to find an excuse not to go. And even if you somehow managed to visit, you might prefer to stand in a corner and do your best to find a way to get out of the place, as soon as you could. That's the mischief of self-image, which governs all your behaviors and actions in a particular situation.

Therefore, your level of action or performance will be limited to the level you see yourself capable of. You would never behave or perform beyond what you see yourself.

Jason Selk, one of United States premier performance coaches, considers **self-image as key ingredient of high performance**. He states: *"Self-image is essentially how you view yourself—what strengths and weaknesses you believe you possess and what you believe you are capable of achieving."* Selk compares self-image to a thermostat and explains how performance can never exceed the self-image you have set for yourself. In one of his books, he stated:

> *Essentially, the self-image governs how successful any individual becomes because it motivates and shapes work ethic and effort. In this way, self-image is like a thermostat. If you set the thermostat at 72 degrees Fahrenheit and the room drops to 71 degrees, the thermostat then sends a message to the heater to get to work. Warm air rushes into the room, and the room warms up to 72 degrees. When the room reaches 73 degrees, the thermostat tells the heater to stop working. All day long, the*

thermostat governs the temperature in the room and won't allow the room temperature to rise or drop from the desired temperature for long.

Human beings are the same: we neither outperform nor underperform our self-image for long. That's why it is so important to set your self-image gauge high enough to achieve your life goals. Set your self-image gauge too low, and by definition, you'll underachieve, because your mind won't call for the motivation to achieve more.

In this light, it becomes really important to first take a close look at how we see ourselves. Once we are able to see ourselves as capable to do a particular task, then our action will be aligned with our identity. As someone rightly stated once: ***"Your identity precedes your activity."***

Okay, what should you do next?

I suggest spending some time in introspection and assessing how you perceive your self-image? Don't assume that your self-image remains the same throughout your entire life. It is rather fluid and keeps on changing subtly and gradually as you grow up and get exposed to different types of environments.

If you think your self-image is not supporting you to deliver performance in your pursuits, then it is time to change your self-image.

One important point here is not to bother about what people think of you. If you realize that your perception of your self is not serving you and not leading you to live the life of your dreams, then it's time to change.

An intriguing rule called the **"18:40:60 Rule"** was coined by Dr. Daniel Amen to highlight how we think erroneously about people and what reality is indeed. It tells us what human beings think about others at different stages in life.

- **When you're 18**, you worry about what the world is thinking about you
- **When you're 40**, you don't give a darn what anybody thinks about you
- And finally **when you're 60**, you realize that nobody's been thinking about you at all

Believe me, I can relate this to myself and it was an really an eye opener for me. I remember clearly when I was about to publish my first book a few years ago, I always worried what other people would think about me. I have a law background and had the impression of people thinking that I should be writing only about law or the business world.

I was continually anxious about how people would think about and perceive me when they came to know that I loved to write personal development books. I was confused whether writing motivational or inspirational stuff was too soft or mystical, or a woo-woo concept for a serious profession like law. But thankfully, I realized that it was all in my own head, and no one is really thinking that much about you.

I love this wonderful quote from Gary Vaynerchuk: *"When you get rid of what others will think about you, you give yourself the gift of speed."*

How do you change your self-image to perform better?

If you realize that you are not able to perform or take charge of your life, it's time to change your self-image.

Yes, it's quite possible.

You have already learned the concept neuroplasticity that supports the idea that your body and brain change.

The principles through which your current self-image is formed, work the same way, when you want to change them for good. The only difference is that earlier you allowed your self-image to build on its own (thanks to outside exposures) and now you have to control the way you want to mold this self-image.

Mental Rehearsal + Personal Statement Technique

In order to change self-image, there was a great technique suggested by Lanny Bassham, an American sports shooter and Olympics gold medalist, in his great book, *With Winning in Mind*. Bassham claims to have spoken to hundreds of Olympic athletes and PGA tour pros about their secrets of high performance. Every one of them had answered unequivocally that **at least 90% of their game was a mental game.**

He offers a formula for changing your self-image through specific mental training. This mental training serves a dual purpose. First, the practice involves personal statements to see you as an achiever, and the second and most important, is about mentally practicing the performance at the highest level. His mental training formula serves this dual objective with two components:

1. Mental Rehearsal

A mental rehearsal in not like a vision board showing a marvelous outcome like grand luxurious homes, fancy cars, or foreign travel, etc.

It is also not about the visualization of you already having achieved desired results. It is about **rehearsing the process of taking action towards getting results**. In this approach, you mentally rehearse performing a task in most effective way and see yourself making the perfect move and succeeding.

To this element of mental rehearsal, you need to add a personal statement.

2. **Personal statement:** *"I do it all the time"* + *"That's Like me"*

Now, this personal statement is a game changer. Such statements do the job of imprinting a new identity of yourself in your mind — an identity of a person who takes action and achieve goals. It is based on the concept of neuroplasticity that says our minds get molded depending upon the environment, behavior, and our thinking and emotions.

In his book, Bassham shares a personal example of how with the help of the mental training explained above, and without much physical training, he was able to win the game. He states that before he won the Olympic gold, he was in the Army. He was stationed somewhere two hundred and fifty miles away from a shooting range. So, in the entire two-year period when he was away from the shooting range, he was only able to shoot for six days, and they were only during competitions — three days for one national competition and three days for another — meaning literally no resources to practice for competitions.

Here is what he did. After his family went to bed, he'd spend two to four hours a night and five nights a week imagining that he was practicing shooting. In this mental rehearsal, he was standing in the correct posture, aiming the point and then finally shooting exactly at the destination. Surprisingly, he won two national competitions with the help of mental rehearsals.

That's the power of building a performer's self-image with a mental rehearsal of your best performance.

Self affirmation

There is another wonderful approach that can help you imbibe any new belief on an autopilot basis. I'm talking about the self-affirmation of beliefs by repetition until the new beliefs become part of your identity.

Let's understand this by way of a metaphor. Before the internet took over the whole world by storm in a span of last few years, we used to have audio cassettes and tapes to listen to music or other audio stuff, followed by the invention of CDs.

One thing about audio cassettes, tapes or CDs was

that you could overwrite those tapes with new songs or audio, which means that the older songs wouldn't exist anymore: rather a new set of songs were recorded and stored, so we could enjoy new songs with a simple re-recording.

It is the same with our minds. When we are born, we really don't know about religion, faith, jurisdiction, or cultural beliefs. Our minds are really blank tapes or CDs in childhood. But then as we grow up, we get imprints of thoughts and beliefs from our parents, friends, society, and the prevailing culture. That means we record the blank audio tapes of our minds with society's thoughts, belief and patterns. Our minds would only play the songs that others recorded on our blank CDs or audiotapes.

Now add one more instance to the above example. Assume you fall in love and get married to someone from a different religion or faith. And since he or she is your partner, you start following certain rituals or adopting practices of that faith in your life. Instead of going to church, you now accompany your partner to a temple or other place of worship where he or she follows these rituals. This is a bit of overwriting or rerecording of new beliefs over the past recording.

But here is the thing.

Why allow imprints to happen only by accident? Why not selectively imprint those beliefs in our minds that are going to serve us by achieving our significant goals and ambitions? Why don't we intentionally choose to create new neural-pathways or patterns that make us capable of thinking and believing differently?

How is that possible? It's through the power of self-affirmation.

Before we continue, let's admit that there is a wrong connotation associated with affirmations. Some people say affirmations don't work; rather, they believe you are getting swayed by some wishy-washy and mystical statements that don't have any connection with reality. I was also skeptical about the effectiveness of affirmations. It felt like I was fooling my mind with false statements that I was repeating blindly, in stark contrast to my reality.

But I realized that the problem was not with affirmations, but with the way these affirmations are crafted. Most self-help gurus will teach you to state affirmations in the present tense, as if you have achieved the success. Like "I'm enjoying the life like a millionaire," while in reality you are just slogging through a low-paying unsatisfying job, or "I'm in the best relationship with my spouse and kids," and the reality is something entirely opposite.

There are many problems with these kinds of affirmations. First, since they don't feel real, you don't believe them. Second, they make you feel as if you don't need to do anything and just give you momentary pleasure until you encounter the real world. Third, they aggravate the level of inner conflict between your current reality and future goals to be attained.

There is a better way through different kinds of affirmation statements that I learned from Hal Elrod while reading his bestselling book, *Miracle Morning*, many years ago. He says that instead of telling your mind statements that appear to be false on the surface and feel like cheating yourself, you should use the affirmation that appear logical and push you forward to take action.

A statement like, "I'm committed to reducing my weight by 20 pounds within 3 months, and therefore, I'm committed to taking all the necessary action including work out, diet etc, that will bring me closer to my ultimate goal" is much better than saying, "I'm already thin and fit currently."

Therefore you should write your affirmation in the form of commitment in the area of life you want to improve. You can write anywhere between 3-5 affirmation in any area of your life that are instantly important for you. Now repeat the self affirmations every morning a few times. With enough rehearsal, you'll start to give a new message to your mind, and soon you'll find yourself changing your behavior and taking action accordingly.

Power up your self-talk

- You are stupid
- You don't how to handle specific things and mess up often
- You don't have what it takes and you won't amount to much

How do the above statements look to you? I remember reading a book some time ago that started with these statements. I stopped for a moment and wondered how could any author speak to his readers in such an insulting way? You too might have thought like this. Yes, I felt a bit angry and shocked, but it also aroused an intriguing urge to know what would happen next in the book.

Thankfully, I read further and here is what I found.

The author wanted to test the feelings that come to our minds when another person says such words to us. We get angry and ready to fight and break the nose of that person (unless the fellow is not in a dominating position in our lives).

But isn't our self-talk like this? Don't we use similar statements while talking to ourselves? In fact, a large majority of the population talk to themselves like this most of the time. We often plague our mindsets with negative self-talk. We fight with outsiders if they say negative about us, but we give more time and promote this negative self-talk. And you can easily guess where this leads.

Do you want to get rid of negative self-talk? Let's look at a formula that will clear these negative thoughts like a strong wind sweeping away dirt. This formula also is known as WIND formula.

The WIND Formula is a four-step process and each letter is an acronym for the respective steps.

W - Witness negative thoughts:

One of the best ways to fight negative thoughts and energy is not necessarily by avoiding them. Rather, progress can be made if you stay detached and become a mere witness to these negative thoughts as they creep into your mind. You start to recognize these thoughts but refuse to be identified with them. If you stay detached long enough, they will stop flowing through your mind and become transformed into positive energy in the long run.

The key to becoming a witness to negative thoughts begins with practicing awareness: being mindful and paying proper attention to the thoughts that cross your mind and the words you speak to yourself.

I - Interdict negative statements:

No matter how hard we try, negative thoughts will find ways to creep into our conscious thoughts. While this is a normal occurrence, it is your responsibility to stop these thoughts once they spring up with a power statement. Interdict means prohibit. It's like preventing an enemy army from entering your territory.

N – Nurture your mind with positive affirmations:

Make it a habit to say positive things about yourself regularly: when you wake up first thing in the morning or as you sit alone with your thoughts on a train or bus ride, etc. Thoughts and confessions will keep you motivated and fortify you against invasive negative thoughts. Moreover, you can write down positive lines that resonate with you that you can place on a wall in your room or on a desk in class or at work.

D – Drive to your new mental state with zeal:

Have you ever heard the statement, "never say never"? This means that no matter the condition or circumstance, always hold your head high and never undermine the potency of powerful affirmations. As we learnt that affirmations are the re-recording of new set of beliefs to overwrite the old ones, and with enough practice and adding zeal and emotions to the affirmations multiplies the power of affirmation. When positive emotions are attached to positive self-affirmations, you speed up the journey of upgrading your self-talk, because our mind registers any thoughts that are powered up by emotions and stores them in long term memory.

Therefore, try WIND formula to continuously sweep the dirt of negative self-talk from your mind and soon you'll start to improve your inner voice that will support you and guide you to move towards your goals with confidence and persistence.

Once you change your self-image and self-talk, you remove the first and biggest barriers to your journey of upgrading your mindset. Without inner resistance to new learning or any doubt about your abilities, you open up your mind to new possibilities.

Now let's move on to the next chapter, where you will learn how to insulate yourself from a negative environment and people who pollute you mind and undermine your self-image and self-talk. You'll also learn how to design the right environment for building a growth mindset.

Chapter 4 Key Takeaways

Before you go out and start to see the world with a different outlook, you need to sincerely look inside and know how you perceive yourself, or how you look at your own self-image. You self-image is the key to your level of performance because the identity in your mind gives impetus to the quality of actions outside.

We give too much weight to what other people think or say about us. But the **rule of 18:40:60** tells us that other people are never much bothered about how you act in your life.

You can change your self-image by **using self-affirmation** in the form of commitment language. Also, you should use the **mental rehearsal and personal statement** technique to upgrade your self-image to that of a performer.

Finally, you need to power up your self-talk. Most of the time this self-talk is all negative about our image and capabilities, and it needs to be addressed to upgrade our mindsets. You can use the WIND formula to overcome negative thinking.

- W - **Witness** negative thoughts
- I - **Interdict** negative statements
- N – **Nurture** your mind with positive affirmations
- D – **Drive** to your new mental state with zeal

Chapter 5: Strategically Design Your Surrounding

****

"Who you spend time with is who you become! Change your life by consciously choosing to surround yourself with people with higher standards"

~Tony Robbins

Let's face a harsh reality. Howsoever hard you try to build a new self-image by setting new beliefs, if the people or environment around are not supportive, you will face a really a tough time.

You know that climbing a mountain requires lots of effort, dedication, the application of strategies and persistence. More than physical, it requires mental toughness. But falling from the mountain doesn't take any effort. Merely by letting yourself drop the ropes, you will be instantly pulled by the force of gravity towards a deep valley.

Similarly, on the personal growth journey, there will people around you who will not support you; rather, they might make fun of or ridicule you for your efforts in developing new habits or behaviors. Your endeavor to improve yourself is like climbing a mountain: it takes time. but gettting affected by unsupportive people and a negative environment is like falling down; and it happens instantly, if you don't safeguard yourself.

Therefore, you need to be careful with such people and any kind of environment that distracts you or pulls you away from the path of a growth mindset.

You now know that backed by neuroscience, the concept of neuroplasiticity works on the principle of changing your environment and behavior, you can change your mind. To put it bluntly, **your mindset can never exceed the mindset of people you generally hang out with**.

Therefore, you need to design your environment to the best possible extent. The environment designing process is done in two ways-

- You need to protect yourself from a negative environment and simultaneously
- You need to structure your day and take the time to infuse more positivity into your life

Let's start with how to deal with a negative environment created by the people around us.

HOW TO DEAL WITH NEGATIVE PEOPLE

Who are negative people? Short answer: they are the people who drain our energy, when we spend (or have to spend) time with them.

The human heart is an intelligent tool (even way more than our brains) and can easily feel the level of energy in the people around us.

You might have realized on your own that after meeting someone, you feel very energetic or peaceful at heart. But there are times when after meeting few people, you start to think pessimistically about your life, your future, about the economy or general environment around you. You tend to blame everyone in the world for anything adverse happening around you. That's the symptom of spending time with negative people, who drain the energy from you.

I admit, you can't run away from negative people all the time, so we need to handle such people in a way that it does not influence our thinking. To be strategic, let's put them into two categories:

1. People we are bound to deal and spend time with and have no choice. These people could be a business partner, colleagues at work, your manager, family, or other close relationships. In most of cases, we have to face these people on a pretty regular basis. Let's call them as our ***mandatory partners***. (Of course if pushed against the wall, one may need to think about whether to keep them as mandatory or not.)

2. People we are not required to deal with compulsorily and regularly. By not entertaining such persons, our work or personal life doesn't stop or come to a total halt immediately. They could be childhood friends, neighbors, distant relatives, colleagues unrelated to work, or clients and customers, etc., let's call them ***Optional partners***.

Let's first take a look at the second category of people, which is much easier to handle, after which we will ascertain how to deal with the most important external factors of our life, i.e., our mandatory partners.

A. Dealing with optional negative partners

The simple solution to dealing with optional partners is to limit your interaction with them. You can limit your encounters to just greetings or an occasional brief discussion on a random topic at social occasions. You might think that if most people around you remain in a negative state of mind, then with this advice you will be labeled as anti-social.

Yes, people might judge your new behavior. But for your own good, you should follow the sage advice that we all know from our childhood days, "Better alone than to be in in bad company."

Still, don't freak out that you are being advised to run away from the world and remain in solitude. There is a great solution to this: **be selectively social**.

We know that humans crave love and belongingness. They need the company of others to thrive. But here is the thing, if you sincerely look around, it would not be hard to come across a few people who have a similar positive approach to life to the one you are willing to adopt. Even if you don't find them physically, in this ever-dynamic internet age, you definitely will find them virtually.

For example, you may search Facebook groups on any topic of interest. You may Google your interest area + forums, and there is a high chance that you will find some community or forum in your interest area. The bottom line is not to stay connected with optional negative partners only for the sake of being socially connected.

Please remember that the consequences of staying with such persons are far more dangerous in the long run as compared to being called *anti-social*. By hanging out with such people, you will end up imprinting negative beliefs in your mind or finding fault in others and blaming everything around you. The result is that you will be less action oriented and behave like a victim of circumstances. The message here is to safeguard yourself from such people. There is a simple rule that can help you identify such people and then decide how much time you want to spend with them.

The 3 Minutes/3 Hours/ 3 Days Rule:

This rule works on the premise that all living creature have an electro-magnetic field of energy around them. There are enough studies in the realm of quantum physics to show that this universe operates in terms of energy, vibration and frequency.

The key is to understand that your body understands the energy fields of other people, by just listening and feeling the vibrations in your body when in close vicinity to different types of people. However, a bit of caution: you have to meet a person without a prejudiced mind, lest you treat that person only with preconceived judgments.

If you keep an open mind and are fully with that person, your body's sensations and vibrations (maybe in the pit of your stomach or elsewhere in your body) will give you signals whether that person is worth spending time with. Here comes the "3 minutes/3 hours/3 days" rule to help you examine the people around you:

1. By understanding the feelings/vibrations in your body, you will get a sensory signal as to what kinds of people deserves just **3**

minutes of your time (**repellant people**). With repellent people, you will get a sense of uneasiness and a negative sensation, and you won't feel like being around with them.

2. There are other quality people around, with whom you might spend **3-hours** over dinner or coffee (**neutral people**). They are people who will provide you with a different perspective and thus broaden your horizon. They are not negative thinkers, but maybe they have different knowledge or a perspective about life in general, and you can simply learn from such people. Your body doesn't exhibit any negative sensation, but it doesn't show any craving to stay with them for a longer time.

3. Then there **are 3-day kind of people**, who you admire so much that you are be willing to spend 3 days with them. You want to attend a weekend conference with them, or they could be quality friends with whom you want to go on a long road trip (**attractor people**). You get a deeper sense of joy and pleasure with such people, as your body sends you signals of loving emotions. Maybe you start feeling your heart melting with warmth when being with them.

The duration of 3 minutes/3 hours/ 3 days is not strict, rather it is symbolic to indicate how our bodies can identify the people who are right for us.

Let's move on to handle a critical segment.

B. How to deal with mandatory negative partners

Don't argue with them. An argument with such persons will further feed and aggravate the negative emotions of the negative person at that moment. When you feel the desire to argue, please remember that in most cases, even if you win the argument, you will feel like a loser, because the amount of energy it takes to win will adversely affect other focus areas. Unless you are a lawyer in court fighting litigation for your client or are in a business negotiation, where your livelihood depends on winning arguments, you'll not gain much from winning arguments with negative people, except to just boost your false ego. However, if you consciously choose not to argue with such persons and concentrate on your other work, the other person will lose all his or her force.

Try this: If you don't argue with such a person, you will have a sense of accomplishment or at least peace of mind that you have saved your energy for better productive work. I am not advocating here to put your point across and just accept what the other person is arguing. Be polite, but firm and if the other person doesn't agree, then no worries, you've nothing to lose except the argument.

The above discussion applies to low impact arguments on random discussions. For life-changing decisions, one needs to be firm and if the circumstances demand it, don't hesitate to break with such mandatory partners at your job or business. (However you should not use the same intensity with key relationships -- a spouse, family, parents -- as they are to be treated with more delicacy compared to others.)

Dilute the negative intensity: Let's look at Jim Rohn's famous quote once more from a different perspective: *"You are the average of the five people you spend the most time with."*

When dealing with negative people, try your best to apply the quote to them and not to you. In other words, do not become the sum total of the negative people around you; rather, they should become impacted by your positivity and motivated to change their behavior. This is specifically for close relations that form your immediate home environment.

If people really close to you are suffering from negativity or pessimism, one of the solutions is to bring positive people or circumstances into their lives to dilute their negative approach.

When such people see a different set of human being beaming with positivity, enthusiasm and a lively approach to future, it might have the impact of breaking old patterns, forcing them to look at life differently. Your close relations might not listen to you, but when they hear other people's views and see them happy and joyful, it might change their perspectives.

Let's understand this with the help of an example of a glass filled with water and thick mud at the bottom. What would you do to clean the water of this glass? The simple solution is to pour clean water consistently in such a way that water keeps flowing out of the glass, until all the muddy water gets out. You will notice that **the more clean water you put in, the more muddy water gets out of the glass' and in no time, you have clear and transparent water.**

The same principle applies to negativity. Depending upon the condition or background of such people, the timeline may vary; but yes, bringing more positive people to associate with these close persons will change their negative mindsets.

THE 33% MENTOR RULE

Tai Lopez, an entrepreneur and investor, in one of his TEDx talk stated a rule called the 33% mentor rule. This rule is all about how should you spend your time with the people in your life. He suggests dividing your available time for interaction into three baskets and then spending 33% of it for each basket separately.

- Spend 33% of your time **with people who are on the lower rungs of progress or behind you in their journey to their goals**. It doesn't mean that you spend time with people who have a fixed mindset or are not willing to grow. Here we are talking about helping those who want to grow in life, but unfortunately don't have access to the right support system.

    As per the rule, $1/3^{rd}$ of your time should be allocated to help such people. Remember, on your journey to progress, you too might have taken support from mentors, so it's your time to grant that suport to the people following you.

- Next, 33% of your time is to be spent with **people on your level who become friends and peers**. They are people who are growing and are on a similar path as you. Each of your friends is getting different types of insights in their life or business, so you can benefit from the life experiences and the wisdom gained by each of you during the process. This cuts short your learning journey through the power of collaboration of efforts of many people, so you don't commit the same

- mistakes as others did.

- The final 33% of your time should be spent with **people who are way ahead of you in terms of the goals you want to achieve in life**. If you have ambitions of growing way more than you can currently fathom in your mind, you need to spend time with people who are multiple times ahead of you. By understanding how their mind works, and how they perform in their day-to-day lives, you'll expose your mind to an altogether different paradigm, which is not at all possible if you choose to stay with people at y our own level.

Unless you are already surrounded with like-minded, growth-oriented people, you can easily find online forums as well as physical meet-up groups in your area. There is platform called www.meetup.com where you can easily locate a group meeting with a common objective like a book lovers club, a runners meet up, personal growth meet-up, etc.

The 33% rule works to **effectively design your environment and divide your time into the right brackets**, so you don't have time to waste time with people whose company will pull you down and hinder your progress.

This rule is a perfect segue to talk about the next strategy of masterminding, which is a formal way of putting the 33% rule in practice.

MASTERMINDING

The concept of masterminding was developed by Napoleon Hill in his famous book, *Think and Grow Rich*. Masterminding is nothing but joining hands and minds with like-minded people, so they can all learn from each other and brainstorm their growth possibilities together. Mastermind group holds each other accountable for the deliverables expected.

Masterminding connects people at different levels of their journeys, and there is something for everyone in each success story, failure, and assesment of ongoing progress, etc. Masterminding primarily helps you stay on track towards your goals, with motivation and support from like-minded people following a similar path on the road of life. It keeps you insulated from all the negative people or circumstances in life. The company of like-minded people helps you consider your problems as an opportunity to challenge yourself and emerge as a winner.

A few key benefits of masterminding:

- a. You get a support system to help you keep stay longer in tough times, as there is the possibility that someone in the group may have already overcome such a situation.

- b. The group is emotionally connected as everyone is on the same journey and really understands the pain of suffering in such periods, so they care for each other.

c. There is a great human connection, as human beings are not magnets. **Here like attracts like** (unlike a magnet where the poles repel each other).

In any pursuit of life, you need a mastermind group. You could be in any business, or trade or you could be any professional i.e. doctor, engineer, accountant, lawyer, architect, etc. You could be a painter, writer, singer, dancer or pursuing another form of art. Whoever you are and whatever you do, the significance of masterminding can never be underemphasized.

Chapter 5 Key Takeaways

To stay on track in developing a growth oriented mindset, you need to be very careful about your surrounding environment and the people you spend time with. More often than not, we have to unwillingly spend time with people who have negative attitude towards life, due to our work, relationships or some other reasons. Here it's important to remember that all your efforts to develop the right mindset will be in vain if you don't insulate yourself from the negative people around you.

There are two types of negative people **(1) optional negative partners** (with whom you will want to reduce spending time) and **(2) mandatory negative partners** (with whom you are bound to spend time due to your work requirements or close relationship.

You can choose to shortlist the right kind of people by using **3-minutes/3-hours/3-days Rule** that will help you identify and categorize people as repellant, neutral or attractor.

When dealing with mandatory negative partners, follow the principle of not getting into arguments and try to make an effort to dilute their negativity by bringing more positivity into your life.

In order to best utilize your time with people, **follow the 33% mentor rule**, where you divide your people time into three categories: (a) helping people who are behind you (b) staying connected with people at the same level and (c) following people way ahead of you in terms of progress in life.

You should **mastermind** with likeminded people to get support from those who will insulate you from negative people, while helping you develop new neural pathways by connecting with growth-oriented people.

Chapter 6: Effective Daily Routines to Empower Your Mindset

****

"Either you run the day, or the day runs you."

– Jim Rohn

Humans are nothing but creatures of their own habits. We do what we do mostly governed by set patterns initially installed by our parents and society, and then we carry them out entirely throughout our lifes. Our mindsets are also framed by a number of routines repeated long enough such that they become our way of operating our lives.

Therefore, to change our mindsets, we need to change our routines. To make this game of leveling up our mindsets a lifetime sustainable proposition: certain new routines and habits need to fitted into our daily lives.

The power of routine can never be understated. Routines take a heavy load off our shoulders, as we don't have to exert willpower to take action; rather, actions becomes wired in our brains in such a way that they happen at the subconscious level.

Do you remember the last time you had to use willpower to brush your teeth? If brushing of teeth, which is nothing but another physical body activity can be made part of daily routine, then why can't we fit in any number of good routines in our lives, by enough practice.

The way you start your day, as you get out of bed, determines the quality of your day. Therefore, it becomes of utmost importance that we give well-intentioned direction to our days, by starting with good routines. A strong morning routine is like a strong, nurtured childhood that paves the way for a results-oriented mature life.

I understand that most people in today's highly-connected virtual world immediately get trapped by the demands of work, the moment they check their emails the first thing in the morning. The moment they open their eyes, they can't stop for a moment to even take a deep breathe, but rush to check their phones, as if the universe will come to sudden halt if they don't. (Oh, come on! The universe was operating pretty well while you were sleeping, so it can also operate without your intervention for some more time).

I am talking about upgrading your mindset to help you get relief from the unnecessary stress and anxiety and put you on a fast track towards your goal. And it requires a different approach. You can't achieve better results if you continue to do the same things over and over again. To put it aptly,

"If you do what you've always done, you'll get what you've always gotten." –Tony Robbins

Albert Einstein went to the extent of defining insanity as continuing to do the same things and expecting different results. Therefore, with the knowledge that human minds are malleable and the awareness that humans potential is unknowable yet limitless, let's get to know some of the morning routines that will help you change your thinking.

Collectively, these morning routines should not take more than a 30-40 minutes of your time everyday, if you are sincere about enhancing the quality of life.

Let's understand each of them with a proper understanding of neuroscience and psychology behind them.

PRACTICE GRATITUDE

What is gratitude? The dictionary meaning of the word *gratitude* is **"the quality of being thankful; readiness to show appreciation for and to return the kindness."**

In other words, gratitude is choosing to look at the brighter side of things and appreciate the positive, instead of complaining about the things you don't have.

In his book, *The User Illusion: Cutting Consciousness Down to Size*, author Ton Norretranders states that our minds are exposed to 400 billion bits of information per second. This is really too much information for the brain to immediately process, so it surfs and sifts data to select the most relevant. And the basis of sifting this information is through the filter we unconsciously place over it by our thoughts.

You must remember that our brains have a natural tendency to keep us surviving. They are designed to keep us safe and avoid any pain and discomfort: they want us to exert minimum effort to save our energy by not taking any action. Also, they scare us from new things and going to uncharted areas that might signal danger. This is how our primitive brain were structured when fear was important to save our lives from wild animals in forests.

And to add to our woes, amid all the information we consume through our days in today's hyper connected digital world, a vast majority is negative, be it the news or other people's behavior. The brain's natural tendency to survive and the negativity of information is sufficient to disturb our filtering mechanism.

Here comes the role of gratitude in setting the filter right.

The practice of gratitude gives a message to the brain that you're thankful for a many good things happening to you, so it adjusts its mechanism. With the revised filter, it lets more resourceful information pass through, which is beneficial for changing your brain for good.

Oprah Winfrey rightly said, *"Be thankful for what you have; you'll end up having more. If you concentrate on what you don't have, you will never, ever have enough."*

Scientific research shows that gratitude impacts our mindsets positively

Harvard researcher, Shawn Achor, author of *Before Happiness,* states that something as simple as writing down three things you're grateful for every day for 21 days in a row significantly increases your level of optimism, and it holds for the next six months.

A study was conducted to determine the impact of the feeling of gratitude on the human brain and mindset. For the study, a team of researchers from Indiana University recruited 43 subjects suffering from anxiety or depression.[12] Half of the group were assigned a simple gratitude exercise — writing letters of thanks to people in their lives.

Three months later all 43 underwent brain scans. During these scans, the subjects participated in a gratitude task in which they were told that a benefactor had given them a sum of money and were asked whether they'd like to donate a portion of the funds to charity as an expression of their gratitude. Those who gave away money showed a particular pattern of activity in their brains. But

---

[12] https://www.ncbi.nlm.nih.gov/pubmed/26746580

that wasn't the most interesting part of the findings. The participants who completed the gratitude task months earlier not only reported feeling more gratefulness two weeks after the task than the members of the control group; but also months later, they showed more gratitude-related brain activity on the scanner.

In short, practicing gratitude seems to kick off a healthful, self-perpetuating cycle in the brain — counting your blessings makes it easier to notice and count them later. *And the more good you see in your life, the happier and more successful you're likely to be.*

Further scientific research has proved numerous benefits of practicing gratitude on your mindset and overall mental health. Here are just to list a few:[13]

- **Improves self-esteem.** A study published in the *Journal of Applied Sports Psychology* found that gratitude increased athletes' self-esteem, an essential component for optimal performance. Other studies have shown that gratitude reduces social comparisons. Rather than becoming resentful toward people who have more money or better jobs — a major factor in reduced self-esteem — grateful

---

[13] https://www.psychologytoday.com/blog/what-mentally-strong-people-dont-do/201504/7-scientifically-proven-benefits-gratitude

people are able to appreciate other people's accomplishments.

- **Increases mental strength**. For years, research has shown that gratitude not only reduces stress, but it may also play a significant role in overcoming trauma. A 2006 study published in *Behavior Research and Therapy* found that Vietnam War veterans with high levels of gratitude experienced lower rates of post-traumatic stress disorder. A 2003 study published in the *Journal of Personality and Social Psychology* found that gratitude was a major contributor to resilience following the terrorist attacks on September 11. Recognizing all that you have to be thankful for — even during the worst times — fosters resilience.

- **Improves psychological health.** Gratitude reduces a multitude of toxic emotions, from envy and resentment to frustration and regret. Robert Emmons, a leading gratitude researcher, conducted multiple studies on the link between gratitude and well-being. His research confirms that gratitude effectively increases happiness and reduces depression.

Sonja Lyubomirsky, a psychology professor at the University of California and a happiness researcher, states, "People who are **consistently grateful** have been found to be relatively **happier**, more **energetic**, more **hopeful,** and report experiencing more frequent positive emotions. They also tend to be more **helpful and empathic**, more spiritual and religious, more **forgiving**, and less materialistic than others who are less predisposed to gratefulness. Furthermore, the more a person is inclined to gratitude, the less likely he or she is to be depressed, anxious, lonely, envious, or neurotic."

Also, as Tony Robbins said, *"Energy flows where focus goes."*

Since mindset is nothing but an outlook of looking at the things and circumstances around us differently, the feeling of gratitude immediately shifts our attention to positive things in life. Once we start looking at the positive things, our energy flows in the direction of taking positive actions in our lives.

How to make gratitude a part of everyday life?

Simple. It shouldn't take more than three to five minutes. As you wake up in the morning, try to name three good things in our life. They don't need to be massive things; they can be small things like good sleep, the comfy feeling of your bed, a cool breeze outside your window, or seeing your partner or kids sleeping and relaxed. These simple things could be reasons for feeling grateful, or anything else you feel good about.

Some people use a gratitude journal, where they write a few things they are most grateful for each day. You can write anywhere, like a simple notebook. Whether you think about it or write about it, the key is to be consistent.

- Write three to five things about which you are grateful every morning.
- During the day, look at the things that are going well in your life and feel grateful for them. This will reinforce the habit.
- Do the same thing before going to sleep.

Practice it and you will start to change your mindset positively and attract abundance and joy in your life. The key is to say thank you from the heart, sincerely and with feeling.

MEDITATION: CLEANSE YOUR THINK TANK

All the problems in your life arise from a lack of clarity in your thinking. Highly successful people with a developed mindset are very careful about clearing their thinking, as it helps them to make quick decisions and take action faster.

Most high-performers do an exercise to disengage themselves from their thoughts at least once per day. They have realized that only when the mind starts getting empty can it attract newer thoughts. The exercise to disengage oneself from one's thoughts and emotions is known under the common term, *meditation*. And, no, I don't mean it in any spiritual or religious sense. Strip away those connotations and what you're left with is a very practical and effective day-to-day life tool.

Tim Ferriss, in his bestseller book, **Tools of Titans,** emphasizes the importance of meditation. He states that one of the most important habits of successful people he interviewed was setting aside daily time for meditation.

He has already interviewed more than two hundred people from diverse backgrounds, including business tycoons, top sports athletes, and the best creative minds around the world, like Arnold Schwarzenegger, Jamie Foxx, Edward Norton, Tony Robbins, Maria Sharapova, Peter Thiel, Amanda Palmer, Malcolm Gladwell and many more. Tim categorically states that one of the most common rituals or daily practices followed by more than 80% of these interviewees is that they have adopted some form of meditation or mindfulness practice in their daily routine – a consistent pattern of a secluded practice to be with their own selves.

Ferriss, who himself is a successful author,

entrepreneur and investors, states the benefits as follows, *"Through 20 minutes of consistent meditation, I can become the commander, looking out at the battlefield from a hilltop. I'm able to look at a map of the territory and make high-level decisions."*

Let's try to understand now how meditation helps change your mindset and outlook on life. It is now properly backed by **scientific research**[14] that practicing meditation helps the human brain and mind better control negative emotions like stress, anxiety, or trauma, and also shows improvement in psychological and physiological aspects of the brain. A few benefits are listed below:

1. In 2011, Sara Lazar and her team at Harvard found that mindfulness **meditation can actually change the structure of the brain**: eight weeks of Mindfulness-Based Stress Reduction (MBSR) was found to increase cortical thickness in the hippocampus, the area that governs learning and memory, and in certain areas of the brain that play a role in emotion regulation and the self-referential processing. There were also decreases in brain cell volume seen in the amygdala, which is responsible for fear, anxiety, and stress; and these changes

---

[14] https://www.forbes.com/sites/alicegwalton/2015/02/09/7-ways-meditation-can-actually-change-the-brain/#78bd55b31465

matched the participants' self-reports of their stress levels, indicating that meditation not only changes the brain, but it changes our subjective perception and feelings as well.

2. One recent study found that **just a couple of weeks of meditation training helped people's focus and memory** during the verbal reasoning section of the GRE (Graduate Record Examinations). In fact, the increase in scores was equivalent to 16 percentile points, which is a major and significant development in itself. Since the strong focus of attention (on an object, idea, or activity) is one of the central aims of meditation, it should help people's cognitive skills on the job.

3. A study by UCLA found that that long-term meditators had better-preserved brains than non-meditators as they aged.

You can see that with so many benefits to the brain and its cognitive abilities, meditation helps to provide the right foundation, or the hardware (which is your brain) such that cognitive skills, start to develop. As a result, you start looking at things from a much better perspective.

Meditation doesn't require any specific structure. You can do it anywhere. The best way to do it is by simply sitting in an undistracted environment for a few minutes a day.

How to Practice mindfulness as a daily routine

You don't need hours of time to get started with mindfulness. You can start with just ten minutes every morning and gradually increase to twenty minutes a day, enough to help you disengage you from your thoughts and look at the world with a renewed perspective.

Mindfulness meditation expert Sam Harris compares meditation to walking on a rope: it's easy to explain but difficult to master; but then goes on to describe the steps necessary for proper mindfulness practice[15].

1. Sit comfortably with your spine erect, either in a chair or cross-legged on a cushion.

2. Close your eyes, take a few deep breaths and feel the points of contact between your body and the chair or floor. Notice the sensations associated with sitting—feelings of pressure, warmth, tingling, vibration, etc.

3. Gradually become aware of the process of breathing. Pay attention to wherever you feel your breath most clearly—either at the nostrils, or in the rising and falling of your abdomen.

4. Allow your attention to rest in the mere sensation of breathing. (There is no need to control your breath. Just let it come and

---

[15] https://www.samharris.org/blog/item/how-to-meditate

go naturally.)

5. Every time your mind wanders, gently return it to the sensation of breathing.

6. As you focus on your breath, you will notice that other perceptions and sensations continue to appear: sounds, feelings in the body, emotions, etc. Simply notice these phenomena as they emerge in your field of awareness, and then return to the sensation of breathing.

7. The moment you observe that you are lost in thought, notice the present thought as an object of consciousness. Then return your attention to the breath—or to whatever sounds or sensations arise in the next moment.

8. Continue in this way until you merely witness all objects of consciousness—sights, sounds, sensations, emotions, and even thoughts themselves—as they arise and pass away.

9. Don't fall.

In addition to a formal seated practice, we can also bring the practice of mindfulness to your daily activities while eating, walking, or talking. For meditation practice in daily life, pay attention to what is going on in the present moment and be aware of what is happening and not live unconsciously. If you are eating, that means paying attention to the food: its smell, how you chew and swallow it. If you are walking, that means being more aware of your body movements, your feet touching the ground, the sounds you are hearing, etc.

Your seated practice meditation supports your daily life practice, and vice-versa. They are both equally important.

Those who are new to the practice generally find it useful to hear instructions spoken aloud in the form of a guided meditation.

There are plenty of apps available these days to help you to do a guided meditation:

One meditation mobile app I have tried is called *Headspace*. It is a guided form of meditation that helps you scan through your thoughts, see your thoughts clearly and get into a state of total relaxation. You can find it for Android as well as an iOS version at the following link: https://www.headspace.com

Another recommended guided-meditation app recommended by people is called *Welzen*, and you may check it out at: https://welzen.org/

JOURNALING

As noted earlier, our minds are exposed to 400 billion bits of information every second. There is lot of information on the internet that says our minds think approximately 60,000 thoughts daily. The irony is that 95% of these thoughts are the same: your mind keeps them repeating over and over again. This means that at any point in time, you have only around 5 to 7 different thoughts going on. If you could capture these thoughts and write them down in your journal, it would clear your head for improved thinking, thus helping you redesign your mindset.

Journaling activates the reticular activating system (RAS) of the brain, a bundle of nerves at the brainstem that filters out unnecessary information so the important stuff gets through. It is not possible for our brains to let in and process a billions of bits of information; hence it deploys a filtering system. RAS is the filtering system that allows only that type of information your mind finds most relevant.

For instance, you would like to buy a new red Honda. Once you start thinking about the red Honda, you may notice more red Hondas on the road. It's not that suddenly people have started buying and driving more such cars, but it is your brain's RAS in play, focusing more on the information your mind perceives as important.

Therefore, when you journal about your goals or desires among other things, you see it in front of you on paper, which in turn activates your RAS, which makes you notice relevant opportunities, otherwise you would miss.

Journaling is considered among the most beneficial kind of writing. One 2005 study[16] found that the kind of "expressive writing" often connected with journaling is especially therapeutic. The study found that participants who wrote about traumatic, stressful, or emotional events were significantly less likely to get sick, and were ultimately less seriously affected by trauma than their non-journaling counterparts.

What should you write in your journal?

In his book *Champion's Mind*, author Jim Afremow talks about creating a Champion's Journal. He suggests asking three questions during journalling process.

- what did I do that was good?
- what need to be done better?
- what changes should I make to become my best?

Hal Elrod, in his book, *The Miracle Morning*, suggests what one can write to start journaling; they are called trigger questions.

- What are you grateful for regarding the previous day?
- What are your specific accomplishments?
- What are your specific areas of improvement?
- What are the top 5 things you must do

---

[16] http://apt.rcpsych.org/content/11/5/338.full

today to take your life to the next level.

To know more about journaling, use this link https://www.robinsharma.com/article/how-to-keep-a-journal from Robin Sharma to get a detailed perspective of journal-writing and what it should contain.

A sleeping and waking up routine to tap your subconscious mind

There is a wonderful technique where you use your mind even during sleep time with ten times greater intensity than your waking time to offer great solutions for your complex problems.

> *"Your subconscious mind works continuously, while you are awake, and while you sleep." ~ Napoleon Hill*

This technique works for any answers you are seeking, including how to catapult your thinking and mindset for good. Thomas Edison used to follow this technique and his mantra was, *"Never go to sleep without a request to your subconscious."*

This technique needs to the **last thing you do at night before you go to sleep, and then first thing in the morning**. Let me explain the technique:

- Before sleeping, sit comfortably for a few minutes.
- Now think about your most important questions for which you are seeking an answer.
- Now repeat the questions with intensity as you can for some time.
- After that, you go to sleep for the night.
- The next morning, once you get up and before you get distracted by the news, social media, emails, or anything else, open your journal – a manual diary or a document on your computer.
- Whatever thoughts come to mind about the important questions you thought about last night, start writing or typing quickly. You have to write whatever comes to mind. Keep writing for 5-10 minutes. These thoughts are emanating from your subconscious mind and probably can be the hidden solutions to the problems you have posed to your subconscious last night.
- While writing, you might start to get thoughts in the form of suggestions like making a phone call to someone regarding a project, making a minor tweak in your work, approaching work or a colleague in a different manner, or communicating in a certain way in relationships you want to work on.
- Write down everything, and the most

important part is to take action on the suggestions you wrote in your journal.

Although a few of you might find this to be on the "woo-woo" side of things initially, don't underestimate the power behind it. There is reasoning here. What happens is that when you put all your questions to the subconscious mind, it starts to connect the dots based on information stored in your long-term memory and experiences, in order to find the solutions to your problems. Maybe it will remind you of a previous experience or some person you met in the past who can help you.

The subconscious mind is very powerful, beyond the imagination, and it works for the duration of your sleep, trying to find answers. As you wake up in the morning, it is ready to provide the solutions to you!

The quality of solutions depends on your level of receptivity to new things. Your subconscious mind can tell you many things, some of which you may find absurd or not so absurd, depending upon the rigidity or flexibility of your mindset.

Joshua Waitzkin,[17] a former chess prodigy and tai-chi world champion who we talked about earlier in this book explains that he follows the above morning routine to tap into his subconscious mind to invite breakthroughs and

---

[17] https://tim.blog/2016/03/23/josh-waitzkin-the-prodigy-returns/

get the full benefit of his sleep time.

This technique is in addition to and separate from your normal journaling, which you do to get clarity about your thoughts. You can keep this in its own section of your journal, or maybe add 5–10 minutes extra to your daily entry that day — whatever works best for you.

DAILY EXERCISE

Our bodies are not designed to be stationary, else God would have made us trees. We are given organs and body parts designed to move around, so there must be some purpose behind it. In fact, in the primitive age, it was our moving ability that enabled us to hunt for food. It also helped us to run away from dangerous animals and protect ourselves in dense dangerous forests.

The Industrial Age created a huge demand for manual labor, and again our ability to move and work with our hands provided food on our table. Then came the Information Age, where our brains became the chief operating officers of our bodies and the requirement of moving our body was heavily reduced. Today, you can sit for hours and still have the ability to earn money. But this approach has taken a toll on our physical and mental health. Cases of obesity, stress, and depression are higher than ever.

It is not only physical and mental health to consider in your quest to upgrade your mindset and tap its full potential. You can't ignore the benefits of exercise. Exercise is not only necessary to keep your entire body healthy by allowing the proper digestion of food, thus generating adequate energy; it is much more important when it comes to nourishing our brains.

John Ratey in *Spark: The Revolutionary New Science of Exercise and Brain* explores comprehensively the connection between exercise and the brain. He states in the book:

"Physical activity sparks biological changes that encourage brain cells to bind to one another. For the brain to learn, these connections must be made; they reflect the brain's fundamental ability to adapt to challenges. The more neuroscientists discover about this process, the clearer it becomes that exercise provides an unparalleled stimulus, creating an environment in which the brain is ready, willing, and able to learn.

A regular exercise regime stimulates the release of positive neurotransmitters, like dopamine (which encourages motivation, attention, and pleasure), serotonin (which enhances learning, mood, and self-esteem) and norepinephrine (which leads to arousal and alertness). The best exercise expedites the production of **BDNF** (brain-derived neurotrophic factor), a protein that Ratey has dubbed "Miracle-Gro for the brain."

In fact, researchers have found that if they sprinkled BDNF onto neurons in a petri dish, the cells automatically sprouted new branches, producing the same structural growth required for learning.

As Kelly McGonigal, a psychologist and researcher, explains, "When neuroscientists have peered inside the brains of new exercisers, they have seen **increases in both gray matter** (brain cells) and white matter, the insulation for brain cells that help them communicate quickly and efficiently with each other. Physical exercise like meditation makes your brain bigger and faster, and the prefrontal cortex shows the largest training effect."

Recently, scientists have also discovered an **"exercise hormone" called irisin**, which is linked to improved health and cognitive function. Researchers found that the part of the brain that responds strongly to aerobic exercise is the hippocampus. There have been experiments conducted that show that the structure of hippocampus increases when you are physically it. Since the hippocampus is at the core of the brain's learning and memory systems, it has memory-boosting effects due to improved cardiovascular fitness.[18]

---

[18] https://www.psychologytoday.com/blog/the-athletes-way/201404/physical-activity-improves-cognitive-function

Furthermore, Michael Gelb in his great book, *Think Like Leonardo Da Vinci*, explains that with a few exceptions, the great geniuses of history were gifted with remarkable physical energy and aptitude. It makes common sense. Seriously, how can you think of getting the best out of life, if you find it difficult to get out of bed?

The above research is enough to convince you that exercising is one of greatest tool to hack the limitless potential of your brain. There is no specific exercise that I can recommend, because everyone is different and has different exercise needs. But here is something simple that anyone can do.

You may either run, jog or do some other kind of cardiovascular exercises that brings your heart to the state of beating faster than its normal pace. Here is how you can meet the exercise requirement from a cardiovascular perspective.

Take 220 beats as a standard parameter and then subtract your age from this number. Whatever number comes up, endeavor to make your heart beat by at least 60% of that number. For example, if you are 30 years old, you should take your heart beat to 114 heart beats per minute (60% of 190 (220-30)) doing good exercise for around 20-30 minutes a day.

Generally, a good exercise regime increases your heart beat to around 80-85% of that number, which is the sign of a healthy heart. The above is a rule of thumb for a normal person. However, if you are suffering from a heart-specific problem, please consult your doctor or other health professional before adding any extreme exercise to your routine.

Additionally, you must do some strength exercises to build your muscles as well. Please consult a fitness trainer or join a gym to understand what works best for your physique and biology. You should get the maximum benefit from your body by releasing resourceful brain chemicals that will keep your motivation high on your journey to develop a better outlook. As they say, a healthy mind stays in a healthy body – so get going and move.

Chapter 6 Key Takeaways

A wonderful life is nothing but a combination of well-structured days lived in rows for a long time. And the structure in our days come through well-designed habits and routines.

If you want to drastically improve your mindset, you need to incorporate certain key habits in your daily life. The following are few important routines that if incorporated in your life will automatize your behavior and empower your mindset:

Gratitude: Always be thankful for what you have and never complain about things you don't have. Being grateful shifts your perspective to abundance (what you have) instead of what you lack (scarcity), and you start to attract more opportunities or the right set of people in your life.

Meditation: A tool to disengage yourself from your thoughts, so you can gain insights of wisdom whispered from your deep inner self.

Journaling: You need to be able to see what's going on in your head on a paper. Journaling helps to bring clarity to all areas of your life, because once you declutter your mind by getting your thoughts on paper, your mind has space to invite new ideas and build better connections.

Exercise: Exercising helps release numerous brain chemicals that help you feel happier and motivated towards taking action. Exercise has the potential to change your state and in the enhanced state of your consciousness, you perceive problems as challenges and opportunity to learn and grow.

Chapter 7: Recoding Your Mindset Operating System

****

"Reading is to the mind what exercise is to the body."

~ Joseph Addison

Our Minds are like the operating system of a computer

Whether you have a PC or Mac from Apple, they function through an operating system; could be Windows or iOS. I use a Windows operated laptop for my work, so I'll use the term Windows OS for the purposes of this analogy.

Our mindset is like an operating system (OS), except for two major differences:

- Windows OS continually updates the software to protect it from bugs and viruses through its anti-virus system. There are regular updates to boost the immune system of software OS and insulate it from any virus or bug disturbances.

- Windows regularly releases its latest version and upgrades its software every few years. These upgrades of the OS take into account the overall developments in software architecture, the best features provided by other systems, and integration with other tools and technologies emerging rapidly through modern-day technological advances.

Now we come to mindset OS. Most people continue to run their lives on outdated mindset operating systems coded by their parents, society, teachers, friends, and overall environment ages ago!

We daily encounter negative inputs in the form of conversations or a news items that evoke fear, anxiety, guilt, or anger that are equivalent to viruses and bugs; and they are haunting our minds on a regular basis. The more we engage with those around us who are already bitten by these bugs, the more our own OS is corrupted by these mind viruses. We don't have our inner anti-virus system in place to insulate ourselves from these infections.

Secondly, for the majority of people, upgrading their system is something they can't even imagine. Why? Because they can't even fathom the idea that their mindset should even require an upgrade. For them, the need to upgrade their system implies that it currently has flaws. The suggestion of upgrading will hurt their egos because suggestions have the implication that they've, so far, been operating with a faulty system. Consequently, they would rather expend most of their energy protecting that faulty system. Sadly, they don't know or don't want to know that they are plagued by a fixed mindset. Since you are reading this book about upgrading your mindset, definitely you don't believe that way.

Now let's talk about how to upgrade or reprogram the operating system of our mindset. How do we do it? It's simply through exposing our minds to new set of information by way of reading.

Why reading is like installation of new code to your mindset

Reading provides you with new material to equip you with a renewed perspective, or a different way of looking at things. It helps you broaden your thinking and view things in a new light, to look at things in a way you hadn't previously considered.

The author of any book, in the process of writing it, distills their knowledge and experience of years of fusing various concepts, and places it in a convenient and easy to consume content form. Therefore, in a way reading a book is like having a conversation over coffee with one of the smart people on the planet. It's difficult to get an appointment from Tim Ferris or Robin Sharma for a one-on-one mentoring session, but it costs a few bucks to consume the knowledge these authors have put in the form of a book. You can't meet Stephen Covey personally, as he is no longer on this planet, but you can still pick his brain through his great book, *The 7 Habits of Highly Effective People*. Books make great ideas immortal.

Furthermore, reading provides you with a new set of data-points that develop new neural pathways and connections in your brain to stimulate your thinking, thus enabling you to become more precise in your approach toward handling of life situations.

You can find various articles that tell you that, on an average, CEOs of big companies read 60 books a year. See the reading habits of ultra-successful people **here**.[19] Bill Gates and Warren Buffett are famous for spending 4 to 5 hours a day reading books. Check out Bill Gates' blog at **www.gatesnotes.com**; you will be amazed to see his library of thousands of books.

In fact, Warren Buffett was once asked about the key to success; he pointed to a stack of nearby books and said, "Read 500 pages like this every day. **That's how knowledge works. It builds up, like compound interest.** All of you can do it, but I guarantee not many of you *will* do it."

See, these people are already icons, and at the apex of success, and still they find time to read. Why? Because it helps carry on sharpening their minds with the newest available knowledge, so that they *continue* to work on their mindsets and adapt to ongoing change. In short, it helps them code their mindsets and make them contemporary and suitable for any changes coming their way.

There is however a notable difference between the reading habits of the wealthy and the not-so-

---

[19] https://www.huffingtonpost.com/andrew-merle/the-reading-habits-of-ult_b_9688130.html

wealthy. According to Tom Corley, author of *Rich Habits: The Daily Success Habits of Wealthy Individuals*, rich people (defined as having an annual income of $160,000 or more and a liquid net worth of $3.2 million-plus) read for self-improvement, education and success, whereas poor people (annual income of $35,000 or less and a liquid net worth of $5,000 or less) read primarily to be entertained.

Successful people tend to choose educational books and publications over novels, tabloids and magazines. In particular, they are drawn to biographies and autobiographies of other successful people for the purpose of guidance and inspiration.

What and How You Should Read

Of course, I won't tell you to read fiction novels be they political thriller, science fiction adventure, or comedy. When we are talking about mindset redesign, you need to read great books about personal development books to understand human psychology and behavior. Reading up on these topics will surely trigger your "action buttons": they will change your behavior and prompt you to take action.

If you pause for a moment and think what you learned from this very book since the introduction up to this page, you might realize that this book is doing the job of opening your perspective on life through stories, real-life example, science-backed findings and practical ways, you can transform your life by implementing my suggested strategies.

Clearly, books are the easiest form of incorporating new knowledge into your brain. And as you know already, neuroplasticity works to redesign your brain, so you must subject your brain to novel concepts and ideas.

When I say *reading*, the intention here is to expose your mind to new knowledge, and that includes listening to audiobooks or podcasts and watching online videos or courses.

Use a JUST-IN-TIME reading approach

It's not advisable to pick any book in general without a specific intention or goal for that reading. Don't just start reading anything, no matter how good it might be, unless it serves your information needs. Instead, it would be more beneficial to consider what kind of specific issues you might need to focus on. You can make a list of issues like this:

- Habit formation
- Being more productive
- Fighting doubts and anxiety
- Developing mindset and personal psychology
- Health
- Relationship
- etc.

Once you have listed your areas of concentration, go one step further. Consider the area that needs the most urgent attention — the area which, if not tended to promptly, might adversely impact all other areas of your life. Start reading books in that area. The *just-in-time* approach suggests picking up recommended books in the area where you want to see improvement faster, and then start reading the one that most closely addresses your needs.

I can't tell you any specific book to start with, as it depends on your personal needs and life situation. But don't think too much, just make reading a part of your habit. Reading biographies or autobiographies is also a good idea to start with, if you love to get immersed in stories and simultaneously learn life lessons.

I've experienced that my entire life, be it personal, professional or as a writer, has been shaped by lots and lots of reading. There was a phase in my life, however, when I couldn't read, and you know what? Those were not the most productive of times of my life and I was rather stressed, anxious and lacking clarity. But somehow, my old habits of reading and learning reasserted themselves and I started getting positive results again. I have been able to make courageous decisions and effect drastic changes in my life with not nearly as much difficulty as one might expect — thanks to books.

How often should you read?

You should read minimum of 15–20 minutes every day and develop this as a lifetime habit. You cannot get benefits by reading just once in a while. You need to get yourself motivated on a regular basis. As Zig Ziglar rightly said, *"People often say that motivation doesn't last. Well, neither does bathing – that's why we recommend it daily."*

Today's generation is the most time-starved generation. So most people might wonder how they can implement reading in their already tightly-packed schedule. Here are a few quick suggestions:

- If you travel by public transport, read while commuting to your office. Instead of watching funny cat videos or consuming too much news, shift your habit to read personal development literature.

- If you drive to the office and can't read in that duration, you still have a solution. Yes, you can consume audiobooks and create a university on wheels, as Brain Tracy puts it. Listening to audiobooks and podcasts was my favorite way of absorbing tons of content, when I was commuting to and from the office in my corporate job days. And to be honest, the traffic jams didn't bother me much, as I was not just traveling, I was in a conversation with some of my favorite authors and learning from them. Good idea, isn't it?

- If you are waiting in a queue for an appointment, you can still read a book in e-book format (yes, you don't need to carry a book with you).

It's not a matter of a lack of resources or time; rather, it's a lack of resourcefulness and prioritization that creates the problem of scarcity of time. If you are convinced that by leveling up your mindset through learning from others, you can design a high-quality life; then the question of finding time for reading will not arise, and you'll squeeze in every opportunity to fit reading into your schedule.

Learning and implementation

However, it's important that to receive the maximum benefit from reading, you must try to implement the teachings as quickly as possible or else you will lose the learning. Let me explain it through one more analogy.

Most of us know that turmeric has positive therapeutic effects in treating various conditions. But some research shows that if you add a little bit of black pepper to the medicinal preparation, it will dramatically improve the results.

So, if you are putting time, energy, and effort into reading this book or any other, please try to implement the same practically in your life situations. This will help you engrain those learnings into your neural pathways, which will only help you remember and take action on whatever you have learned. After all, what is the use of all that learning, after all, if you can't implement and get improvements in your life as a result?

Therefore, you should endeavor to implement the learning through changing your behavior; it will soon become part of your psychology and rewire you brain by designing new neural pathways. You'll learn much better by implementing the ideas in your life.

Chapter 7 Key Takeaways

You can't change your mindset if you continue to repeat the same thoughts in your head. You need to **expose your mind to resourceful information regularly** to rewire your brain and see things from different perspectives.

Your mindset is like **an operating system of a computer** that also get infected by the bugs and viruses of negativity from people around you. Also, your outside world is continuously spreading new information and events, so you need to develop compatibility and adapt to changes around you for your own good.

You should not read just anything, rather your reading needs to be intentional with a specific objective. Use the **just-in-time approach** when learning anything new. Set a specific learning goal and then shortlist the learning material accordingly.

Make it a **habit to read 15-20 minutes a day**. It might be less, but with daily incremental progress, a compound effect comes into play; and over time, you will develop a renewed mindset. Also, focus on **learning and implementing simultaneously** in your day-to-day life.

Chapter 8: Accept Challenges + Make Mistakes = Robust Mindset

****

> *"The brick walls are there for a reason. The brick walls are not there to keep us out. The brick walls are there to give us a chance to show how badly we want something."*
>
> *~ Randy Pausch*

When exercising in a gym, I remember reading a poster affixed on one of the walls, showing a bodybuilder doing push-ups. Underneath the image was a wonderful quote by the legend, Muhammad Ali, *"I don't count my sit-ups; I only start counting when it starts hurting because they're the only ones that count."*

What an inspiring statement.

You would also agree that anything monumental, before its grand shape takes form, requires a lot of pain and pressure to accomplish. In fact, pain and pressure are the key prerequisites to master anything.

"No Pressure, No Diamonds", as beautifully said by Thomas Carlyle. If your mindset is weak and afraid of trying anything new outside its zone of comfort, it will get hurt and experience pain. Therefore, your mind will find all sorts of excuses not to do it.

At the end of the day, all the assorted self-help and motivational literature available (like this book!) are here to aid and encourage people who often get stuck due to a lack of courage or because they are plagued with over-thinking.

But the people who consistently take action get life lessons and the next steps directly from the actions themselves. They get the next signals one after the other. Their actions make them stronger. They, of course, also encounter difficult problems and go through tough periods, but instead of freezing in fear under such circumstances, they choose to take it head on and *work through* the fear.

Because, as David J. Schwartz rightly said, *"Action cures fear."*

Every high performer will tell you that the real magic lies beyond the comfort zone. Only your willingness to accept challenges and do the things that scare you will ultimately give you the wherewithal to take your life to the next level.

It's only by taking action in the face of fear that you develop confidence. The journey has milestones as follows:

Fear >> Courage>> Competence

>>*Confidence*

Fear is a basic trait and a necessary part of existence. In fact, in the initial evolutionary stage of mankind, being afraid was a necessary part of survival. Our brains are designed to keep us safe and in survival mode. As stated earlier, fear is generated in a specific portion of the brain called the *amygdala*. The amygdala helps to trigger in your body a sense of danger and threat to life, immediately alerting you to take action.

In our more primitive stage of development, when humans were living in forests and the fight for survival was a rather constant and pressing affair, man was guided by these fear neurons to safeguard his life. Fear sent an instant message, prompting *fight* or *flight*. If man didn't have this fear response, he would have been easily killed by a predator such as a tiger or lion.

Today, of course, the situation has drastically changed for the better. We have developed for ourselves a very safe physical environment, as compared to those very early years of human history. There is less probability that we will be subjected to life threating things at a moment's notice. But our minds have still not evolved fully enough to rid ourselves of that fear entirely. The difference is that the things we fear now come in a different form. Now, fears are of a different nature:

- What if I fail?

- What will people think about me?
- I have not done it before, so I won't be able to do it now.
- etc.

So, coming to the point, how do we tackle this?

Join the COURAGE gym!

Courage is your mental gym. Here you have to put pressure on your mind with the weight of fears.

Some people wrongly think that courage is a lack of fear. Instead, it is other way round. Courage is standing in front of fear and taking action. Once you face more and more fear, despite being scared, you start developing your courage muscles.

After you have developed enough courage muscle, your confidence will begin to take shape. Confidence is a lack of fear. Doing similar things many times develops your competence and skill. You start to feel that you can do it. And, so, you *can* do it.

Consider J.P. Sears, who runs a very popular YouTube channel named, "How to be Ultra-Spiritual." He has taken the seemingly serious topic of spirituality, but deals with it in a hilarious way. I was listening to a podcast interview, where he explained how terrified he was to try taking such an important topic as spirituality and combining it with humor. He was afraid that it might offend people's sensibilities. He was fearful of looking foolish. His fearful mind was telling him that he should speak seriously when presenting and discussing spiritually.

Despite all this internal mental chatter, he forged ahead and created some darned funny videos, taking YouTube by storm, and gathering more than 100 million views in only a short amount of time. So, you could say his endeavor was a success!

Make Mistakes to Improve Your Thinking

"A man's mistakes are his portals of discovery."
~ James Joyce

People are scared of committing a mistake, as if heaven would fall, if they commit one. But this fear of committing mistakes is a major stumbling block in learning to take action and thus improve your mindset.

In fact, mistakes are growth stimulators, because they indicate that you have taken some action even if that action didn't show the right result. It means you have closed one wrong door and now are open to something new.

Thomas Edison once rightly opined about committing mistakes and failure when he said, *"I have not failed. I've just found 10,000 ways that won't work."*

Mistakes mean that you are shifting from taking an imaginary action and failing in your mind to real action on the ground through which you will learn a real lesson in life. The problem of taking action in your mind is that you can't fathom how uncertain and unknown factors will play out in reality. These real factors will show up only in real time in the physical world, which is outside your mind. You can think in your head, but you can't act in your head. **While thinking happens in the head, real action happens on real ground.**

But here is the thing, the more you make mistakes, the more you'll learn as it will change your neuro-circuitry based on experience.

It's not merely philosophical advice to learn from mistakes; **neuroscience has established that our brains are self-aware when they commit a mistake.** As reported in an article[20], Andy Wills, a psychologist at the University of Exeter and his team conducted research on a group of volunteers to test how their brains registered mistakes and learned to correct them. The participants were required to make predictions about the answers to a few questions on a computer screen. Once they made their predictions, they were shown another screen that illustrated many of those predictions as incorrect.

---

[20] https://www.livescience.com/7312-study-reveals-learn-mistakes.html

The objective the research was to see how the human brain reacts when it realizes its mistakes. The study proved that as soon as the participants looked at the second screen, their minds realized the mistakes in fractions of a second. The lower portion of the brain immediately sends signal to the whole brain about the mistake in milliseconds so that the mind wouldn't commit the same mistake in the second round.

This study shows that the human mind registers mistakes quickly, even before it reaches the conscious thinking portion of the brain. It shows that the mind has the capacity to quickly learn from mistakes and register them in memory.

Committing mistakes at least moves you forward from your current situation to the next level. You either achieve results or come to know the faults in your approach. You gain both ways: ether you achieve your goals or else you learn the right ways to do it.

John W. Gardner aptly said: *"We pay a heavy price for our fear of failure. It is a powerful obstacle to growth. It assures the progressive narrowing of the personality and prevents exploration and experimentation. There is no learning without some difficulty and fumbling. If you want to keep on learning, you must keep on risking failure - all your life."*

And George Bernard Shaw stated, *"When I was a young man I observed that nine out of ten things*

I did were failures. I didn't want to be a failure, so I did ten times more work."

Avoid blunders, but don't bother about mistakes

Keep in mind, however, that there is a difference between a mistake and a blunder. Don't be frightened of nor discouraged by making mistakes. But be careful not to make a blunder! What is the difference between a *mistake* and *blunder?*

A mistake's effects are not drastically endangering, and it is something that can be easily reversed at a minor cost or with minimal time. So, a mistake can be corrected in short order. A blunder, on the other hand, is something catastrophic. It is like jumping off a cliff knowing that you will almost certainly die, or if you survived, you would have the hardest time recovering.

So, start small. Do things that are a bit scary at first, and increase the intensity gradually. With every action you take, you will open your mindset and further broaden your thinking horizon.

> *"What you are afraid to do is a clear indication of the next thing you need to do."~ Ralph Waldo Emerson*

One caution regarding mistakes

Life is too short to commit all mistakes on our own. If you can learn from others' mistakes, trying new things that will be better.

Warren Buffet once said, *"It's good to learn from your mistakes. It's better to learn from other people's mistakes."*

Choose to Deal with Setbacks in a Way that Keeps You Focused on the Big Picture

It is one thing to learn from mistakes, but when your efforts don't give you the desired results, you might get disheartened and slip into pessimistic thinking if not handled properly.

So, how exactly should you deal with setbacks that you know will happen? You need to be prepared mentally. In other words, you have to believe that setbacks, disappointments, failure, and rejection do happen. But they don't have to be permanent. They don't have to rule out your future: you can work around them. You have to deal with setbacks. Don't allow yourself to be surprised and to get emotionally drained by the experience.

Snap into your fallback position

You have to have some sort of **fallback position** when you get knocked back. In wrestling, when wrestlers get hit—skilled wrestlers don't avoid these hits. Instead, they learn how to take them.

In other words, they have a fallback position so when they get hit, they don't fall flat on their backs. They fall in a certain way or assume a certain position that allows them to spring back. You should do the same mentally and have certain fallback positions when the worst outcomes happen.

If you get disappointed or are facing a nasty setback, you can do the following:

You can choose to learn. This is always a good idea. Or you can choose to actively find an alternative route. You know that the door ahead of you has closed. There are no two ways about it: it is beyond dispute. You say to yourself, "Okay, I'm going to move on. I'm going to accept this." But you start looking for an alternative. This is your personal GPS. It tells you in that pleasant voice, "recalculating route."

Another fallback position **you could take is to change your sub-goals**. Remember, a big goal is actually made up of subsidiary goals that lead to the big one, just as a big belief is made up of smaller assumptions that lead to the big belief. So change these elements.

Another thing you can do is **to redirect your resources**. Maybe the reason you failed is because you did not give it 100%. You split your attention and resources between two or more projects. This is your opportunity to redirect your resources to where they need to go so you can achieve greater success.

Regardless of which options you choose, you need to allow yourself to get pumped up by your setbacks. When you allow yourself to get engaged by a setback and excited by it, this proves you are trying. You're not screwing around; you're not just hoping and wishing; you're actually trying.

Finally, you have to wrap your mind around the possibility that it's only a matter of time until you achieve a breakthrough.

With an upgraded self-image, powered up self-talk, surrounded by high-quality environment further bolstered by effective daily routines, you are ready to take on the life challenges with a positive attitude.

With the help of effective tools, you can take challenges as opportunities and failure as a teacher; you can learn better from practical life situations and yes, you have put yourself to the journey of upgrading your mindset to keep evolving as the best version of yourself.

Chapter 8 Key Takeaways

To strengthen your mindset, you need to expose it to challenging situations and face them despite being fearful.

Courage is not lack of fear; rather, it is **taking action despite fear**. The formula to transform your fear into confidence is:

Fear >> Courage >> Competence >> Confidence

Studies show that our minds are pretty amazing at noticing mistakes and they don't repeat them the next time. So take advantage of this ability of the mind and don't be afraid of mistakes. By committing mistakes, you close the wrong doors faster and soon you will get on the right path.

You never fail, you either win or you learn. You **shouldn't be afraid of committing mistakes**, though be careful of committing blunders. As Warren Buffett said, you should also **learn from the mistakes of others** as well.

When facing adverse life situations, always **maintain yourself in a fallback position**, the way wrestlers do. You shouldn't fall in a way that you won't get up again. Rather, fall back with the intention to get up sooner than later. A fallback option requires you to either taking lessons from failures or redirecting your resources in a more organized way while changing the sub-goals that will drive you to your main ones.

Final Words...

"Old ways won't open new doors." ~ Unknown

Here we reach the end of our journey together. Maybe it was for a few hours or a few days. Whatever the time, I thank you for your interest and investing time and energy in yourself.

I have said enough about what you can do to change your mindset in this book. Now a last parting piece of advice: **"don't stop here."** Don't let this book become just another digital compilation or get stashed on your bookshelf. Go out and try the things you've learned.

Be crazy. It doesn't matter what people will think of you. Build yourself to be strong from the inside, insulate yourself from negative people while you design your dream environment. Develop great habits and routines to fill your days. Be courageous and take action to build a resilient and robust mindset.

It's your life, and you know that you can design it the way you want. Don't live your life based on what others have told you, but rather steer your own ship. Remember this quote:

> ***"I am the master of my fate. I am the captain of my soul."***
>
> **~ William Ernest Hanley**

Now start taking action to redesign your mindset. I wish you all success in your endeavors and an amazing life ahead.

Cheers.

May I ask you for a small favor?

At the outset, I want to give you a big thanks for taking out time to read this book. You could have chosen any other book, but you took mine, and I totally appreciate this.

I hope you got at least a few actionable insights that will have a positive impact on your day to day life.

Can I ask for 30 seconds more of your time?

I'd love if you could leave a review about the book. Reviews may not matter to big-name authors; but they're a tremendous help for authors like me, who don't have much following. They help me to grow my readership by encouraging folks to take a chance on my books.

To put it straight– **reviews are the life blood for any author.**

Please leave your review by clicking below will directly lead you to book review page.

CLICK TO LEAVE YOUR REVIEW HERE

It will just take less than a minute of yours, but will tremendously help me to reach out to more people, so please leave your review.

Thanks for your support to my work. And I'd love to see your review.

Full Book Summary

Introduction Key Takeaways

There can be any worst of worst life situation, but with right mindset to look at the circumstances, one can deal with situations as challenge and design their life. At the same time, with lack of right mindset, one would always feel like a victim of circumstances and out of control of their lives.

Mindset is the **manner in which you look at the things** that come your way- **your perspective of the people and situation** around you- **the lens** you put on your eyes to see the world around.

With an upgraded mindset, you will benefit in all areas of your life, be they financial, relationships, personal growth, social circle or any other aspects of life.

This book will offer you a recipe to **shift your perspective by first designing your inner world and then designing your outer world**, so you can take the challenges head and make the most of it, and ultimately become the captain of your own ship.

Chapter 1 Key Takeaways

Humans have always demonstrated tremendous potential in terms of their physical capability as well as thinking ability.

Physically, human can run hundreds of miles in one spurt, climb Mount Everest without any support or break any myth about the human's body's false limits.

In terms of **thinking,** the vastness of human potential is beyond the imagination. People like Elon Musk are trying to make space travel for humans possible. There are plenty of examples of people who have succeeded wildly despite adverse life situations by keeping a positive mindset.

The examples you read in this chapter exemplify the quote by T.S. Eliot, **"Only those who will risk going too far can possibly find out how far one can go."**

The future is unknown and there will always be endless possibilities for anyone who develops the right mindset and is willing to learn and explore.

Chapter 2 Key Takeaways

Your brain and mind can be compared to computer hardware (like the CPU, monitor screen, keyboard, etc.) and software (like Windows or iOS, Microsoft Office, etc.), respectively.

The brain is your physical hardware with billions of neurons, responsible for coordinating your moves, various physiological processes, and day-to-day activities.

The mind is the manifestation of thought, perception, emotion, determination, memory and imagination — that all take place within the brain.

Mindset is a particular way of thinking about circumstances, events or people based on your own unique position or perspective. It's a setting of the mind, a lens or frame of mind through which we view the world.

Therefore, while *mind* is a combination of thoughts and perceptions in general, *mindset* is a particular attitude toward actions and beliefs.

There are two types of mindsets:

Fixed mindset: people with this mindset believe their intelligence or mental abilities are fixed traits and therefore cannot be changed. Failure for them means they don't have what it takes to succeed. Putting effort into something means wasting time.

Growth mindset: people with a growth mindset have an underlying belief that their learning and intelligence can grow with time and experience. Failure means the opportunity to learn and grow and putting in effort means they can master any skill they want.

You **shouldn't label your child as smart and dumb**, as it makes him or her behave according to the label. Instead of labeling in a particular way, tell the child about the behavior that will make him or her achieve success in life.

Listen to your divine angel (big thinking) and don't pay attention to your little devil (small thinking) to strengthen growth mindset. It will help you take action, learn and grow to become the best version of yourself.

You can test your mindset type on a scale by answering the simple questionnaire given in the chapter.

Chapter 3 Key Takeaways

Modern history is filled with examples of legends, who despite their unfavorable childhoods or even less than average beginnings, turn out to disrupt the world with their genius.

Therefore, the concept of "born genius or else no hope" is a myth. Instead, in the words of Michael Gelb, *"Geniuses are made not born."*

Research and the invention of brain imaging technologies like the fMRI have proven the incredible morphing abilities of the brain. The concept of neuroplasticity proves the **ability of your brain to reorganize itself, both physically and functionally, throughout your life due to changes in your environment, behavior, thinking and emotions**.

As per Lara Boyd, you can change your brain at the chemical, structural and functional level. The real-life incident in the chapter shows how 50% of your brain can handle 100% of your brain activities, thanks to the reorganizing abilities our brain.

Your brain makes physical changes based on the repetitive things you do and the experiences you have. Therefore, you need to do specific activities or design new behavior to change your mindset.

The following are the **5 pillars to build a robust mindset** to upgrade your mindset:

6. **Self-image and self-talk** (inner mastery)

7. Redesigning your **surrounding environment**

8. Automating a mindset upgrade by **effective daily routines**

9. **Recoding a** new mindset operating system.

10. **Toughening your mindset** to become

resilient

Chapter 4 Key Takeaways

Before you go out and start to see the world with a different outlook, you need to sincerely look inside and know how you perceive yourself, or how you look at your own self-image. You self-image is the key to your level of performance because the identity in your mind gives impetus to the quality of actions outside.

We give too much weight to what other people think or say about us. But the **rule of 18:40:60** tells us that other people are never much bothered about how you act in your life.

You can change your self-image by **using self-affirmation** in the form of commitment language. Also, you should use the **mental rehearsal and personal statement** technique to upgrade your self-image to that of a performer.

Finally, you need to power up your self-talk. Most of the time this self-talk is all negative about our image and capabilities, and it needs to be addressed to upgrade our mindsets. You can use the WIND formula to overcome negative thinking.

- W - **Witness** negative thoughts
- I - **Interdict** negative statements

- N – **Nurture y**our mind with positive affirmations
- D – **Drive** to your new mental state with zeal

Chapter 5 Key Takeaways

To stay on track in developing a growth oriented mindset, you need to be very careful about your surrounding environment and the people you spend time with. More often than not, we have to unwillingly spend time with people who have negative attitude towards life, due to our work, relationships or some other reasons. Here it's important to remember that all your efforts to develop the right mindset will be in vain if you don't insulate yourself from the negative people around you.

There are two types of negative people **(1) optional negative partners** (with whom you will want to reduce spending time) and **(2) mandatory negative partners (**with whom you are bound to spend time due to your work requirements or close relationship.

You can choose to shortlist the right kind of people by using **3-minutes/3-hours/3-days Rule** that will help you identify and categorize people as repellant, neutral or attractor.

When dealing with mandatory negative partners, follow the principle of not getting into arguments and try to make an effort to dilute their negativity by bringing more positivity into your life.

In order to best utilize your time with people, **follow the 33% mentor rule**, where you divide your people time into three categories: (a) helping people who are behind you (b) staying connected with people at the same level and (c) following people way ahead of you in terms of progress in life.

You should **mastermind** with likeminded people to get support from those who will insulate you from negative people, while helping you develop new neural pathways by connecting with growth-oriented people.

Chapter 6 Key Takeaways

A wonderful life is nothing but a combination of well-structured days lived in rows for a long time. And the structure in our days come through well-designed habits and routines.

If you want to drastically improve your mindset, you need to incorporate certain key habits in your daily life. The following are few important routines that if incorporated in your life will automatize your behavior and empower your mindset:

Gratitude: Always be thankful for what you have and never complain about things you don't have. Being grateful shifts your perspective to abundance (what you have) instead of what you lack (scarcity), and you start to attract more opportunities or the right set of people in your life.

Meditation: A tool to disengage yourself from your thoughts, so you can gain insights of wisdom whispered from your deep inner self.

Journaling: You need to be able to see what's going on in your head on a paper. Journaling helps to bring clarity to all areas of your life, because once you declutter your mind by getting your thoughts on paper, your mind has space to invite new ideas and build better connections.

Exercise: Exercising helps release numerous brain chemicals that help you feel happier and motivated towards taking action. Exercise has the potential to change your state and in the enhanced state of your consciousness, you perceive problems as challenges and opportunity to learn and grow.

Chapter 7 Key Takeaways

You can't change your mindset if you continue to repeat the same thoughts in your head. You need to **expose your mind to resourceful information regularly** to rewire your brain and see things from different perspectives.

Your mindset is like **an operating system of a computer** that also get infected by the bugs and viruses of negativity from people around you. Also, your outside world is continuously spreading new information and events, so you need to develop compatibility and adapt to changes around you for your own good.

You should not read just anything, rather your reading needs to be intentional with a specific objective. Use the **just-in-time approach** when learning anything new. Set a specific learning goal and then shortlist the learning material accordingly.

Make it a **habit to read 15-20 minutes a day**. It might be less, but with daily incremental progress, a compound effect comes into play; and over time, you will develop a renewed mindset. Also, focus on **learning and implementing simultaneously** in your day-to-day life.

Chapter 8 Key Takeaways

To strengthen your mindset, you need to expose it to challenging situations and face them despite being fearful.

Courage is not lack of fear; rather, it is **taking action despite fear**. The formula to transform your fear into confidence is:

Fear >> Courage >> Competence >> Confidence

Studies show that our minds are pretty amazing at noticing mistakes and they don't repeat them the next time. So take advantage of this ability of the mind and don't be afraid of mistakes. By committing mistakes, you close the wrong doors faster and soon you will get on the right path.

You never fail, you either win or you learn. You **shouldn't be afraid of committing mistakes**, though be careful of committing blunders. As Warren Buffett said, you should also **learn from the mistakes of others** as well.

When facing adverse life situations, always **maintain yourself in a fallback position**, the way wrestlers do. You shouldn't fall in a way that you won't get up again. Rather, fall back with the intention to get up sooner than later. A fallback option requires you to either taking lessons from failures or redirecting your resources in a more organized way while changing the sub-goals that will drive you to your main ones.

Could you please leave a review on the book?

One last time!

I'd love if you could leave a review about the book. Reviews may not matter to big-name authors; but they're a tremendous help for authors like me, who don't have much following. They help me to grow my readership by encouraging folks to take a chance on my books.

To put it straight– **reviews are the life blood for any author.**

Please leave your review by clicking below will directly lead you to book review page.

[CLICK TO LEAVE YOUR REVIEW HERE](#)

It will just take less than a minute of yours, but will tremendously help me to reach out to more people, so please leave your review.

Thank you for supporting my work and I'd love to see your review soon

Preview of the book "Level-up Your Self Discipline"

Introduction

****

"With self-discipline, all things are possible. Without it, even the simplest goal can seem like the impossible dream."

~ Theodore Roosevelt

My Personal Experience

"Hey, it's already 7:45, and you're still at home. You'll find the school door closed for sure today, and we'll have to apologize the school principal to let you in," my wife screamed at my daughter again in the morning. "Why don't you get up bit early, despite me trying to wake you up ten times?" she continued with frustration.

Quite frankly, this wasn't the first time for us. It happens quite often, as my thirteen-year-old daughter needs to wake up early in the morning to reach her school by 8 a.m.

When I dropped her off for school, my daughter was sad about the morning's scolding.

"Hey Dad, why does mamma get angry with me only in the morning? It spoils my day. And it's really difficult for me to wake up in the morning despite trying hard," she complained.

As any father would, I tried to explain her, "Don't think negative about your mamma's words, rather try to understand that it's not a good idea to be late for school, and then request school authorities to let you in the building. The best thing to do is to go to bed earlier, get enough sleep, and then wake up in the morning refreshed. It is all a matter of maintaining some discipline in your sleeping schedule. That's it."

She retorted, "Come on, Daddy. None of you at home sleep early, and I am told to sleep early. How can I do it alone?"

Her answer hit me like a ton of bricks. I suddenly realized that I was expecting my thirteen-year-old daughter to wake up earlier, while there was a lack of discipline on my and my spouse's part as parents. I was not creating an environment where lights would switch off by 10 p.m. every night, so my kids could get enough sleep and start the next day better.

This is nothing but a lack of self-discipline. And I assume this might be an experience common among most parents.

In case you don't have children at home, or live alone or with your friend or better-half, you might have a different situation that requires exercising some kind of self-discipline.

Maybe you prefer sitting in front of the TV watching late-night shows until 2 a.m., despite having to wake up at 6.30 a.m. and get ready for work. Even if you know that you have to prepare for a Monday morning presentation for a crucial meeting with one of your firm's important clients, and you are stressed too, still you stay up late Sunday nights binging on TV shows.

Perhaps you are overweight but unable to resist your temptation to chow down on giant-sized burgers, pizzas, or sweetened highly-carbonated beverages, despite being aware that lack of control is only adding to your woes.

Or in case, you smoke, you already know (in fact, every smoker knows it) that cigarette smoking is injurious to health. Even cigarette companies are mandated in most of the countries to put a big warning sign on each pack, stating "cigarette smoking is injurious to your health", with images of dreadful consequences, people suffer. Or maybe your doctor has told you to avoid smoking or drinking for the sake of your health, but despite your good intentions, you generally give in— merely at the sight of cigarette or alcohol.

One can go on and on and cite many such instances, where people lack self-control. They don't have the willpower to resist the temptations of eating, drinking, and entertaining, which may put all their future at a stake.

Lack of Willpower- Barrier to any Change

American Psychological Association conducts an annual nationwide survey to examine the state of stress across the country and understand its impact on its people. In 2011, this survey reported[21] that 27% of the respondents complained that a lack of willpower was the most significant barrier to the change.

So the big question is, why aren't we able to resist temptations, despite being rational and grown up people?

What You Will Discover in This Book

This book is all about explaining the human psychology and neuroscience behind our irrational behaviours and actions, triggered by our emotions, and how can we use different strategies to mould our behavior with a few simple tweaks and improve the quality of our days and lives.

You will understand the power of self-discipline in accelerating your growth to shape your future for better, as has been proven by scientific studies conducted by researchers.

---

[21]

http://www.apa.org/news/press/releases/2012/02/willpower.aspx

You will explore deeper into human psychology to understand why you do what you do. The book will explain you why people get tripped off and succumb to temptations despite being aware of consequences of their self-defeating behaviours. You will then learn how certain extraneous factors are responsible for draining your willpower and the ways to overcome them.

If you are sincere about mastering self-discipline you will learn the four key tenets followed by Navy SEALs to build mental toughness. You will also learn how by only instilling only a handful of mini habits, you can start working without any need of willpower—and be on autopilot mode.

This book is not merely a general advice book; rather it is filled with psychological research conducted by renowned researchers, who spent decades in researching the concept of willpower. Also, the scientific studies in this book will help you to understand the root behind your particular behaviours, and how you can build self-discipline with proven principles and by implementing effective habits.

And now without further ado, let's get started.

Chapter 1: Self-Discipline: The Engine of Success

****

"The one quality which sets one man apart from another— the key which lifts one to every aspiration while others are caught up in the mire of mediocrity—is not talent, formal education, nor intellectual brightness—it is self-discipline."

~ Theodore Roosevelt

Willpower and Self-Discipline Defined

Let's start by understanding the concept and meaning of *willpower* and *self-discipline*.

While **willpower** is the ability of your mind to keep itself under control, **self-discipline or self-control** is the action of consistently doing or avoiding something despite distracting temptations.

According to most psychological scientists, as reported by the APA[22], willpower can be defined as:

- The **ability to delay gratification**, resisting short-term temptations in order to meet long-term goals.
- The capacity **to override an unwanted thought**, feeling, or impulse.
- The ability **to employ a "cool" cognitive system** of behaviour rather than a "hot" emotional system.
- Conscious, effortful regulation of the self by the self.
- A limited resource capable of being depleted.

Collins Dictionary defines self-discipline as the ability to control yourself and to make yourself work hard or behave in a particular way without needing anyone else to tell you what to do.

To put it in simpler terms, self-discipline helps you take control your thoughts, emotions and behaviour, and empowers you take action in a particular way (that directs you in a positive direction or stops you from going in a negative direction).

Roy Baumeister, a social psychologist at Florida State University and a researcher on willpower,

---
[22] http://www.apa.org/helpcenter/willpower.aspx

describes **three necessary components for achieving your goals**:

1) First, you need to establish the **motivation for change** and set a clear goal.
2) Second, you need to **monitor your behaviour** toward that goal.
3) The third component is **willpower**. Whether your goal is to lose weight, kick a smoking habit, study more, or spend less time on social media, willpower is a critical step to achieving that outcome.

How Willpower can Change the Trajectory of Life

As we all know, a solid building requires a rock solid foundation. That applies to planning and structuring our lives, too. The robust foundation of our childhood ensures that we become smarter and stronger adults. Self-discipline is one of the most important skills, which, if developed sooner in life, will help in almost all areas of life, be it health, finance, relationship, or career. One study conducted decades back has already shown how self-discipline mastered in early childhood helps to achieve growth in all areas of one's adult life.

The Marshmallow Test

If you are not brand new in your exploration of the concept of self-discipline, you might have already heard about the famous marshmallow test case study. In almost any discussion on the willpower and self-control, you will invariably find this research and discussion, as this research showed some powerful effects of self-discipline on the overall well-being of humans. This test was conducted in 1960s by psychologist and researcher Walter Mischel, who did a study on school kids to test their self-control. Here is how the test was conducted:

A group of pre-schoolers were made to sit in the room. The researcher offered each of them a marshmallow. But before they could gulp that sweet candy, the researchers offered them with two simple choices:

1. They could eat one marshmallow immediately; or
2. Those who could wait for the researcher to come back after twenty minutes, would get two marshmallows instead of one.

It seems like a rational choice to wait just twenty minutes and then get two marshmallows instead of one. Looks like a simple maths, isn't it?

But here is what actually happened.

After giving this choice, the researcher went out of this room, leaving children with their marshmallows, but he started watching the kids from a one-way glass window to see how the children would react in this situation.

As you might have guessed already, kids are kids. Some of them couldn't wait and instantly swallowed their marshmallow and were very happy. But there were few others, who behaved more rationally. These children calculated: two marshmallows merely by a wait of twenty minutes. They resorted to focusing on other things to divert their attention from the one marshmallow lying in front of them in order to resist their temptations. These children exercised their willpower to delay the instant gratification in order to get a bigger reward.

But this research did not end here.

Researchers continued to follow these pre-schoolers not for years, but for decades. In a 2011 study[23], they tracked the 59 subjects, then in their forties, who participated in the marshmallow test as children. It was noted that the **children who were able to resist their temptations and had delayed the need of instant gratification were able to score higher SAT scores, get better grades, were more focussed, and were way more successful** as compared to those who failed in the marshmallow test.

You can see how inculcating self-discipline from an early age helps to create a better future in adults in almost all areas of their lives.

- [23]. https://www.ncbi.nlm.nih.gov/pubmed/21876169

Additionally, the researchers **tested the brain activity** in the subjects by use of function magnetic resonance imaging (fMRI) technique. When presented with tempting stimuli, individuals with low self-control showed brain patterns that differed from those with high self-control. The researchers found that **the *prefrontal cortex*, a region that controls executive functions, such as making choices, was more active in subjects with higher self-control**. And the *ventral striatum*, a region that processes desires and rewards, showed boosted activity in those with lower self-control.

Let's also look at a few more studies conducted that also showed how delaying instant gratification proved to be a real game changer for people.

Get One Dollar Now or Two Dollars Next Week

This study[24] was conducted at the University of Pennsylvania by psychologists Angela Duckworth and Martin Seligman on a few eighth grade students. During the test, the students were given the option of receiving one dollar immediately or waiting a week to get two dollars the next week.

---

[24] http://journals.sagepub.com/doi/abs/10.1111/j.1467-9280.2005.01641.x

This was again a test of how the students can delay their instant gratification and control their temptation for a larger reward in future. The researchers noted that the **students who demonstrated more self-discipline had performed much better in their studies, got good grades, got admission to highly ranked universities**, as compared to their counterparts who had lesser self-control. In this study, the researchers also concluded that **self-control was more important than the IQ** of the students in getting into good schools or getting better jobs.

A New Zealand Study

Another study[25] conducted in Dunedin, New Zealand that also demonstrated that the benefits of willpower extended well beyond the college years. In this study, researchers took a control group of 1,000 people for a long-term health study, who were **tracked from birth until thirty-two years old**.

The researchers noted that by ten years old, many children had mastered self-control, but others were failing to achieve this skill. Then, researchers followed them over a period of thirty years and traced the consequences of their childhood levels of self-control on their health, wealth, and possible criminal offenses.

---

[25] http://www.pnas.org/content/108/7/2693

The research concluded that **individuals who had a higher self-control during childhood, as reported by their teachers, parents, and the children themselves, became adults who had much better physical and mental health**. They were also better off financially. They also concluded, based on court convictions and police records from New Zealand and Australia that children with poor self-control were more likely to be convicted of a criminal offence.

All of these studies are clear evidence that resisting short-term temptations, and overpowering the desires for instant gratification for a better future by exercising willpower proved to be highly advantageous in the lives of people.

Strengthen Willpower to Redesign your Life

Let's list down some of the key benefits that you can get by strengthening your willpower muscles:

- You can **prioritize your work**. Self-discipline gives you a confidence that you can commit yourself and continue to take actions towards your long-term goals. You know that with self-discipline, you are not a slave to your temptations, you know that you can stay committed to your goals longer, and therefore, significantly increase the chances of achieving your goals.

- You **feel a sense of accomplishment**. Through the power of self-discipline, you don't drift from your path. You stay focused and therefore start getting results sooner, which gives you a sense of fulfilment and further boosts your morale and confidence.
- You **feel in command of your life**. You know that whatever actions you decide, you will stick to those plans and work longer and progress faster. You feel like you're in the driver seat of your life and not merely a victim of your circumstances.
- **Self-discipline brings freedom**. It seems to be counterintuitive, but if you can manage your time well by exercising self-control, you increase your focus on your work. You can finish your work faster, more effectively, and this gives you the freedom to spend your saved time with your family or friends or on activities that you enjoy most.

And this was rightly said by a wise philosopher, **Aristotle**:

- *"Through discipline comes freedom."*

- You **improve your relationships**. Through enhanced willpower, you improve your relationship with yourself and the people around you. You see yourself in control of your life as a whole, and this empowers you with quality time to think and act. Since you are not stressed or anxious, you look at the situations and people more compassionately and listen with empathy, and therefore you develop and improve your relationships with others.

- **You get out of your own way.** More often, it is our own negative and distracted thinking that deters our progress. Enhanced willpower helps us to stick to our guns in the difficult times, and gradually, we are able to conquer our inner critic, which is one of the most dangerous obstacles on our way to success.

- You can **control your behaviour**. Willpower strengthens you to take a tougher stand during tempting situations that can otherwise derail you from your path and can adversely affect your progress. You can better sail through this situation with self-discipline and can even get rid of your addictions.

In this section, you learned about why self-discipline is such a powerful weapon in your armoury that can help you win any situation of your life. It is an engine for your success. But despite knowing that we can improve our lives through self-discipline, why do we often get tripped up and lose discipline?

--End of Preview--

Get your copy of the full book here >>>

Level-Up Your Self-Discipline: Understand the Neuroscience of Self-Discipline, Control Your Emotions, Overcome Procrastination, and Achieve Your Difficult Goals

My Books in <u>Personal Mastery Series</u>

1. **<u>Mindset Makeover</u>**: *<u>Understand the Neuroscience of Mindset, Improve Self-Image, Master Routines for a Whole New Mind, & Reach your Full Human Potential</u>*

2. **<u>Level-Up Your Self-Discipline</u>**: *<u>Understand the Neuroscience of Self-Discipline, Control Your Emotions, Overcome Procrastination, and Achieve Your Difficult Goals</u>*

3. **<u>Trigger High Performance:</u>** *<u>Upgrade Your Mind, Learn Effectively to Become an Expert, Activate Flow State to Take Relentless Action, and Perform At Your Best</u>*

Copyright © 2020 by Som Bathla

All rights reserved. No part of this book may be reproduced in any form without permission in writing from the author.

No part of this publication may be reproduced or transmitted in any form or by any means, mechanical or electronic, including photocopying or recording, or by any information storage and retrieval system, or transmitted by email or by any other means whatsoever without permission in writing from the author.

Printed in Great Britain
by Amazon